# THINKING
about water in uncertain times

Sailen Routray | N. Shantha Mohan

# THINKING about water in uncertain times

state, people and conflicts

AAKAR

THINKING ABOUT WATER IN UNCERTAIN TIMES

Sailen Routray and N. Shantha Mohan



First Published in 2020

ISBN 978-93-5002-607-6



Published by
AAKAR BOOKS
28 E Pocket IV, Mayur Vihar Phase I,
Delhi 110 091, India
www.aakarbooks.com

Editor: Samprati Pani
Typeset by Dsgn Unplugged, dsgn-unplugged.blogspot.in

Printed at
D.K. Fine Art Press, Delhi

*We dedicate this work to the faculty, post-doctoral fellows and doctoral students at National Institute of Advanced Studies (NIAS) and the institute's Directors, whose engagement with it has shaped its contours.*

## CONTENTS

# PREFACE

This book is a collection of six essays by the authors on conflicts around water, some written individually and the others co-authored. These essays are based on their work facilitated through their affiliation with the Water Programme at National Institute of Advanced Studies (NIAS), Bangalore. Professor N. Shantha Mohan led this programme as a faculty at NIAS, while Sailen Routray contributed towards the work as a doctoral candidate at the institute. Research in this programme has included interstate transboundary water sharing and conflict resolution, the formation of zonal water partnerships (ZWPs), and the development of interdisciplinary knowledge in relation to transboundary water sharing. The aims of this work have been to develop context-specific multidisciplinary knowledge on social, economic, cultural, legal and political aspects of water sharing and conflicts.

A version of the chapter titled 'The Water Sector in India: An Overview` was published in the edited volume *River Water Sharing: Transboundary Conflict and Cooperation in India* (Routledge, 2010). It discusses the various sectoral usages of water in irrigation and domestic use for drinking purpose, and two issues of contemporary relevance–the deepening crisis of groundwater and the river interlinking project. It then analyses some emerging approaches to water issues, such as integrated water resource management (IWRM) and water pricing in the market mode. This essay also deals with various aspects of water conflicts and their resolution including various constitutional mechanisms and institutional reforms. A variant of the chapter 'Locating Transboundary Water Sharing in India` by N. Shantha Mohan was published in the same volume brought out by Routledge. This chapter discusses both national and international level cooperation, institutional mechanisms and rules with respect to transboundary rivers.

The chapter titled 'Water as an Ethic: Three Ways of Talking about Water and Rights` first appeared in a slightly different version in the edited volume *Sharing Blue Gold: Locating Water Conflicts in India* (NIAS, 2015).

A variant of the chapter 'Securing Livelihoods: Emergence of the "Social" in a Watershed Project in Odisha` was first published in *Indian Journal of Human Development* (2012). It provides a review of the relevant social science literature on watershed development in India. Drawing upon fieldwork undertaken in a participatory watershed development project in Kalahandi in Odisha, it tries to establish interlinkages between the emerging importance of livelihood-related concerns in watershed development and the ways in which this new focus is related to, what this essay calls, the emergence of the 'social` as a site and trope of governmental action.

The volume *Reinventing Public Management and Development in Emerging Economies* (MacMillan Publishers India Ltd, 2011) carried a version of the chapter titled 'Sarkar in the Backyard: State Fabrication in a Watershed Project in

Kalahandi`. Drawing upon ethnographic fieldwork in the state of Odisha, this essay argues that doing watershed development work in the mission mode, as opposed to the work on watershed development done by the soil conservation department, allows for new institutional assemblages. This helps the governmental apparatus to reach deep into hitherto marginal rural areas and population groups, which has had important impacts on the ground regarding the functioning of the state and the way it is perceived by people.

The essay titled 'Interstate Transboundary Water Sharing in India: Conflict and Cooperation` was first published in a slightly different form in 2012 by Academic Foundation in the volume *Perspectives on Water: Constructing Alternative Narratives*, edited by Lydia Powell and Sonali Mitra. It discusses conflicts and cooperation over the sharing of transboundary rivers in India between the states, and the rules and mechanisms to address transboundary water sharing in the country, such as the Interstate River Water Disputes Act of 1956. It then goes on to explore the Inter-State Council, formation of river basin organizations, mediation and scenario building as probable institutions and tools for conflict resolution with respect to transboundary water sharing and conflicts.

1

# THE WATER SECTOR IN INDIA

## An Overview

*Sailen Routray*

India has only 4 per cent of the world`s water resources even as it has around 16 per cent of the world`s population and 2.45 per cent of its land. In gross national terms, the availability of water in India is not inadequate right now. This situation can, however, change with population growth, economic development and increasing urbanisation. There are of course many problems with aggregates at the national level. India, as the cliché goes, is a land of wide variations in terms of most issues, and this extends to the water sector as well. With respect to water availability, there exists a wide range of both spatial and temporal variations. Most of the precipitation in the country happens through rainfall, which is received in the four months between July and October in most parts of the country as a result of the southwest monsoon. Spatially, broadly speaking, the northern and eastern parts of the country have better water endowments compared to the western and southern. The less endowed parts include the desert areas of Rajasthan and the arid areas in the states of Gujarat, Maharashtra, Karnataka, Andhra Pradesh and Tamil Nadu in peninsular India that lie in one rain-shadow region or the other (Iyer 2003).

## SECTORAL USAGE OF WATER

Although water availability in India is spatially and temporally variable, there is a consistency in terms of the patterns of demand. Irrigation is the biggest consumer in all Indian regions, accounting for more than 80 per cent of all water consumed. Domestic usage (including drinking water) and industrial usage together constitute less than 20 per cent of all water demand (Iyer 2001a). Since irrigation is the single biggest consumer of water in the country, it needs to be looked into in some detail.

### Irrigation

The discourse on irrigation in India is largely around surface irrigation, though groundwater is an increasingly significant contributor. Over the last three decades or so, India has seen a massive expansion of groundwater irrigation. There has been a progressive decline in the water table in most areas, and this has led to farmers deepening wells in a competitive manner. This has consequently led to higher costs of irrigation that are being increasingly borne by the poorer farmers. Urban water demands for both domestic and industrial purposes have spiralled upwards during the same period, with a bulk of this demand being met through the exploitation of groundwater. Lack of treatment of effluence has contributed to the pollution of the existing groundwater stocks. Degradation of groundwater through over-extraction and pollution is increasingly contributing to inequity, conflicts, indebtedness and poverty (Janakarajan and Moench 2006).

Surface irrigation projects were important in providing irrigation water till about 1970. From the early 1970s, the rate of expansion of groundwater irrigation has been higher than that of surface water irrigation. The expansion of groundwater has sometimes been able to extend the benefits of irrigation to areas hitherto unreached by surface irrigation systems. It is also a much more efficient source of irrigation as there are fewer evapo-transpiration losses, and it allows farmers better control of both the timing and quantity of water. But due to unsustainable growth over the last decade or so, the groundwater irrigation economy might end up collapsing under its own weight (Shah 2004).

In terms of the existing surface-based systems, there have been no major initiatives to improve the efficiency of water use through renovations. Till now, the attempts at promoting water-use efficiency by inducing institutional changes have neither been concerted nor influential in terms of their impact. In India, the proportion of the irrigated area transferred to water users' associations (WUAs) is around 7 per cent; this compares very unfavourably to 45 per cent achieved in Indonesia, 66 per cent in the Philippines and 22 per cent in Thailand. While institutional changes may hold greater promise in the long term, in the short term, technological changes resulting in improved crop yields per unit of water, inducing farmers to switch to water-efficient crops by pricing mechanisms, the use of rain water in conjunction with irrigation water in high-rainfall areas and greater focus on the high-rainfall areas of central and eastern India might be more promising as strategies. Increasingly, the role of the government in irrigation systems is seen as a part of the problem, leading to the prescription of market mechanisms as the solution. But as experience has more often than not shown, market failures in water and irrigation management are as common as the failure of state systems. There is a widespread prevalence of externalities, high transaction costs and lack of clear property rights for irrigation water in India. This makes it difficult to have properly functioning water markets and any large-scale or full-scale privatisation of irrigation water difficult and potentially inequitable (Hanumantha Rao 2002).

### Drinking Water

Although irrigation is the biggest consumer of water in India, the most important usage of this resource is for drinking and other domestic purposes. Despite the gains made in the water and sanitation sector after independence, tens of millions of people in India are yet to gain access to safe drinking water. About 15 lakh children under the age of five die every year in the country due to preventable, water-borne diseases, and about 20 crore persondays are lost annually (mostly by the poor and the vulnerable) as a result of such diseases.

In 1991, urban water supply coverage was 83.63 per cent, which was an increase of only 10 percentage points over the figure in 1981. Instead of trying to achieve international standards in terms of water and following the targets of total sanitation, various governments have chosen to lower the standards, with the Five Year Plan documents periodically revising targets. The Eighth Five Year Plan (1992–97) set the target of 100 per cent coverage of safe drinking water in urban areas by 2000. After this plan period, the approach paper to the Ninth Plan (1997–2002) claimed that only 85 per cent of the urban population had access to safe drinking water and admitted to inadequate coverage in slums and other poorer localities. The distribution of water in urban areas is extremely inequitable and is biased against the poor. The leakage of water in the big cities of India averages between 35 and 40 per cent; reducing leakages can augment supplies with minimal additional investment (Ramachandraiah 2001).

One of the key players in the emerging policy consensus surrounding urban drinking water across the world has been the World Bank, which has been promoting public–private partnership models based on management contracts. In most such contracts, much of the risks are supposed to be borne by the governments (primarily in developing countries), while the companies more often than not are not required to invest anything. A few years ago, the Delhi state government adopted a similar model for pursuing so-called reforms in the water sector. This was met with widespread protests and led to the unconditional withdrawal of the loan application by the Delhi Water Board to the World Bank (Bhaduri and Kejriwal 2005).

Despite the commitments of successive governments for providing full drinking water coverage to all rural habitations, many villages still lack access to safe drinking water. A large proportion of the so-called no-source villages that are provided with drinking water invariably revert back to the no-source status. This may be because of biophysical factors, but it has to be kept in mind that 'no-source` is as much a political category as it is a technical category. In some cases, villages with sources of drinking water try to get themselves declared as 'no-source` so as to access governmental schemes for rural drinking water provisioning. The seventy-third amendment to the Indian Constitution gives panchayats the power of providing drinking water in villages. Panchayats need to be strengthened financially and institutionally so that they are able to fulfil this constitutional obligation. Most attempts at providing water for the no-source villages have generally attempted to provide water through tankers or pipe water schemes. Attempts should be first made to make villages self-sufficient in drinking water by watershed treatment and similar other measures. If all measures fail, water supply from outside the village or the panchayat can be considered as the last resort.

## TWO ISSUES OF CONTEMPORARY RELEVANCE

Till now, intersectoral conflicts surrounding water usage have not been significant in India. But that does not mean there have been no important conflicts over water resources. Over the last couple of decades or so, the water sector has been an important site of conflicts and contestations. At the macro level, big dams and water resource development projects have been important sites of conflict between many types of social actors. Similarly, the increasingly scarce groundwater resources have been important sites of contestation, albeit at a much less intense level, in many regions of the country. These need to be looked into in some detail.

### The Conundrum of Groundwater

Most of the demand for both irrigation and drinking water till recently was being met with surface water resources. In the last three decades, groundwater has become increasingly important, and its use has been growing at a faster rate than surface water resources.

The first large-scale attempt to scientifically plan and develop groundwater in India was made in 1934. The actual expansion of groundwater irrigation started in 1965 after the introduction of high-yielding varieties of seeds. Increasing availability of electricity in the rural areas due to the rapidly expanding rural electrification programme and the increasingly easier availability of credit due to the growth of the rural cooperative credit structure have helped rapidly increase the number of wells and increase the reach of groundwater irrigation. Over the last few decades, there have been increasingly sophisticated investigations of groundwater resources in the country, though some problems with methodology remain. The methods employed have included hydro-geological surveys, geophysical studies and exploratory drillings (Jain et al. 1977).

The rates of extraction of groundwater in India exceed by multiples the replenishment rate in many blocks, which is leading to a continuous lowering of the water table. In 2004, an alarming 28 per cent of the groundwater blocks in India could be classified in the category of semi-critical, critical or overexploited; the comparable figure in 1995 stood at only 7 per cent. Most recent legislations by some state governments lack any nuanced understanding of the resource—these rely mostly on controls and licenses imposed by the state and have limited scope for community participation. As is evident from experience, both the state and the market seem to find it difficult to ensure the equitable and sustainable use of groundwater. The only option left seems to be management through local community-based institutions that are adequately supported by research. In this context, enabling legal frameworks and well-defined rights also assume importance (EPW Editorial 2007).

### Water Resource Development and the River Interlinking Project

As is evident from the preceding discussion, ground water use in India has already met its limits. Creation of surface water potential in India also seems to be plateauing. With a rapidly growing economy, demand for water can only increase at a faster pace than in the past. This calls for a holistic approach of both demand-side and supply-side management. However, traditionally, the planning for water in India has focused on discrete, individual projects. Projects have almost always been approved on the basis of the benefit–cost ratio (BCR), which is an inherently unsatisfactory criterion and is prone to being distorted. Most of the major and medium projects are loss-making propositions for the various state governments. The costs and benefits of these projects are unevenly distributed across various social groups, and this makes rehabilitation and resettlement a huge problem, as India has one of the worst records regarding these issues. There are also immense problems in terms of the planning, funding and construction of major and medium water resource development projects in the country: these include the thin spread of finances over a large number of projects resulting in cost and time overruns, the persistent overestimation of benefits and underestimation of costs, ignoring social costs and provision of adequate funding for rehabilitation and resettlement, the persistent underestimation of negative environmental impacts, and the substantial and consistent underutilisation of the irrigation potential created (Iyer 2001a).

In the background of such a history of the experience of large water resource development projects, the proposed river interlinking project (RIP) needs to be rigorously examined. The proposal to link all the rivers in India is an old one. The present round of discussions and activities surrounding the plan have started with a writ petition filed in the Supreme Court of India following which the Court treated this issue as an independent public interest litigation (PIL) writ petition. A preliminary analysis indicates that even if the decision were to be based on purely 'technical` matters, then the RIP will lose out to other emerging technological solutions such as desalinisation for meeting drinking water needs of coastal cities or improvements in the realisation of existing irrigation potential for meeting additional irrigation needs. This project is purportedly an attempt at hydraulic equity at the national level that envisages transferring water from the so-called surplus areas to the so-called deficit areas. The inherent logic is flawed on many counts. First, the deficit areas are not necessarily poor or deprived; the deficit has arisen due to a process of intensive water usage in the first place. Second, the promotion of 'national` equity between regions or states would involve heightening social inequities within them between various social groups. Since there have been no professional assessments of the proposals, or even proper pre-feasibility studies, the proposal seems unacceptable on socio-economic and ecological grounds (Bandyopadhyay and Perveen 2004).

One of the major initiatives in this proposal is about building huge storage capacities. Sedimentation of reservoirs is a big problem in India; generally the inflow of actual sedimentation is more than 200 per cent of the design inflow (Tejwani 1987).

A major part of the proposal of the RIP envisions damming the Himalayan rivers. There is a serious absence of long-term records of water flows, and there are practical problems in maintaining data quality, leading to high uncertainty levels in the assessment of water resource potential in these rivers (Kattelmann 1987). The so-called surpluses in the Himalayan rivers must be properly assessed before any major river diversion scheme is planned based on insufficient data.

## NEW APPROACHES AND THEIR LIMITATIONS

Due to the limitations of the water resource development paradigm mentioned in the preceding section, the last few decades have seen the growth of many alternative approaches. These approaches try to respond to the problems that the earlier paradigm either created or failed to address. These include piecemeal and engineering-driven approaches to water resource planning, a lack of focus on environmental and social concerns, and the focus on supply-side rather than demand-side management.

### Watershed Development

Watershed development is an alternative way of dealing with these concerns. The last decade has seen a critique of statist resource management practices and increasing decentralisation of responsibilities for natural resource management to the community level. The watershed development programmes (WDPs) that are being supported by the Government of India are an example of such a change. Assessment and evaluation approaches for judging the success or otherwise of WDPs in India have evolved over a period of time. During the 1970s and early 1980s, the evaluation of WDPs was premised mainly on biophysical criteria. This started changing in the late 1980s with a growing recognition of the fact that watershed development involves more than just maintaining or improving the quality of natural resources and now has objectives related to social, ecological, environmental and equity concerns as well (Turton 2000).

There is increasingly the diagnosis that the 'dryland blindness` of planners and policymakers has failed to recognise that climatic and livelihood uncertainty is an integral part of the lives of people in the drylands occupying much of the country. It is argued that policymakers and planners are based in distant capitals, and they are better accustomed to wetter areas with perennial rivers and more efficient irrigation facilities. They tend to use yardsticks suitable for wetter areas to evaluate and plan water resources, resulting in 'dryland blindness` and the spread of conditions of acute water scarcity in the dryland areas of the country. Rainwater harvesting techniques are probably the best way to tackle the water problem in drylands. The 'dryland blindness thesis` argues that water harvesting is unlikely to have the negative effects associated with large dams and schemes that tap finite groundwater resources. Yet it has not gained acceptability amongst key decision-makers in water resource management. The lesser visibility of watershed development schemes and the lack of appeal of watersheds to powerful business lobbies may explain why watershed development has not been taken up as a political issue (Mehta 2000).

The actual experience of watershed development projects in India has been varied. With a history of at least three decades, these programmes have been conceived basically as a strategy for protection of livelihoods of people living in fragile ecosystems that experience soil erosion and moisture stress. Although the performance of these programmes across various states is highly uneven, their overall performance in the country has shown a distinct improvement after the new guidelines have been in place (Hanumantha Rao 2000).

But such narratives of 'success` do not go uncontested. For example, a water audit conducted as part of the Karnataka Watershed Development Project (KAWAD) shows that demand for water, induced by watershed 'development`, is slowly outstripping supply, and the possibility of augmentation is limited. The audit also found no evidence that watershed development activities have reversed or even halted degradation of water resources or have helped take steps towards making villages drought-proof. Watershed development is not necessarily going to lead to either sustainable or equitable development of natural resources in the KAWAD watersheds (Batchelor et al. 2003). Therefore, watershed development, even in its 'participatory` incarnations, cannot be used as a general panacea for the ills plaguing the irrigation sector in India.

### Traditional Water Management Systems

India has had many different kinds of traditional water management systems, which evolved in response to local needs and conditions. In much of peninsular India, tanks have been important sources of irrigation. But their importance has been decreasing slowly in the post-independence period. The proportion of the gross cropped area irrigated by tanks decreased from nearly 17 per cent in 1952–53 to around 5 per cent in 1999–2000. This has to be seen in conjunction with the fact that the proportion of the area under tank irrigation has decreased more rapidly in states where tank irrigation used to be more important, while the decrease is much less steep in those states where it used be less important. In fact, there have been marginal gains in tank irrigation in states that traditionally relied less on it. Data from the Agricultural Census of India across two decades from 1970–71 to 1990–99 shows that lands of small and marginal farmers owning less than two hectares of land continue to account for the majority of the tank-irrigated area in India. In 1970–71, these two categories together accounted for around 40 per cent of agricultural land irrigated by tanks, a figure which increased to more than 55 per cent by 1990–91. During the same period, the share of large farmers in tank-irrigated areas decreased from around 14 per cent to 6 per cent. Thus tank irrigation remains a crucial resource for small and marginal farmers (Palanisami 2006).

In the last few decades, there has been an increasing recognition of the importance of what are called traditional water harvesting systems that primarily consist of tanks in much of peninsular India. The work of the New Delhi–based research organisation Centre for Science and Environment (CSE) has been crucial in such a refocusing. Tank-based systems in peninsular India have received increasing attention from both academics and practitioners. There has been an increasing recognition of the various state authorities regarding their importance, and over the last decade, there have been many state-sponsored tank rehabilitation programmes. But the actual number of tanks rehabilitated remains proportionately small compared to the total number of tanks. Augmenting tanks through people`s renovation is increasingly seen as a cost-effective as well as equitable tool to address concerns surrounding agricultural productivity and rural poverty. Both physical and institutional measures are necessary for revitalising tanks. In most tank revitalisation programmes, structural improvements tend to overshadow investments in institutional improvement. Before any investments are made in tank-irrigation systems, the availability of adequate water for the tank must be ensured. Enabling institutional preconditions should be created so that tank management institutions are genuinely representative and equitable (Sakthivadivel et al. 2004).

### Integrated Water Resource Management

Integrated water resource management (IWRM) is part of a host of a new set of strategies being promoted by international bodies as innovative practices in the water sector. Indian water policy discussions are generally influenced by overarching global discourses. The discourse surrounding IWRM reflects an emerging global consensus surrounding water; the main elements of this consensus are a naturalised and absolutist notion of water scarcity and its links to poverty and deprivation, and a host of demand management practices and policies. There are serious flaws in such a diagnosis and prescription, the link between water scarcity and 'water poverty' being tenuous. The main components of IWRM packages, such as reforms in water pricing for water to reflect its 'production costs' and the enforcement of water withdrawal permits, have generally been difficult to implement. Attempts at 'integrated planning' at the regional level have failed in a similar manner. One of the main reasons for such failures has been that water economies in poor countries are more often than not informal in nature, and this makes the operation of formal demand management systems that are imposed from above almost impossible to succeed. But IWRM cannot be completely rejected. It has its applications in highly formalised segments of the water economy. With increasing urbanisation, our cities with a significant part of their water economy in the formal sector will need the direct demand management practices as envisaged by IWRM (Shah and van Koppen 2006).

Even in the rural sector, with increasing water scarcity, well-regulated water markets seem to have emerged in certain regions. In these cases also, IWRM can be a fruitful framework to locate interventions for producing desirable outcomes with respect to both equity and efficiency. As a framework, IWRM cannot be rejected summarily without figuring out its applicability in specific sectors and regions. Till very recently, the water sector has been dominated by supply-side concerns and by the various disciplines of engineering. IWRM provides us with a framework to integrate social science concerns with engineering know-how and to address demand-side management. This is a welcome development, and IWRM should be given a fair, if limited, trial as a framework for locating water-related interventions in the country.

### Water Markets and Appropriate Pricing of Water

Due to the apparent inefficiencies in state-managed irrigation systems, market-based mechanisms are increasingly being promoted as alternatives. There are two broad sets of reasons that are given for preferring water markets over administered pricing. Theorists advocating market mechanisms for allocating water resources generally claim that it might be a theoretical possibility to devise and implement an efficiently administered price system, but in the real world, the information requirements are demanding and can hinder the effective functioning of such a system. An administrative solution presumes neutral, efficient and incorruptible administrators and administrative bodies that design and implement the 'correct` prices. More often than not, this is not borne out in practice. These administrative bodies are more often than not captured by interest groups or are ill-informed about future demand or are inefficient and are unable to set and send out the correct price signals or collect the water charges effectively (Mohanty and Gupta 2002). These are, in short, some of the main arguments given for water markets.

Critiques of free-market solutions argue that in actual experience, water markets need regulation and the enforcement of private rights, and they run into the same set of problems as administrated pricing. More importantly, there are many examples of market failures, and the introduction of water markets is no guarantor of an efficient mechanism for allocating water. The informal water economy of countries like India involves complexly intertwined claims over water, and market mechanisms cannot be simply grafted over these. Questions surrounding water equity also assume salience in the context of water markets. In this context, communitarians provide a third alternative to statist and market mechanisms, one that gives effective rights to communities to manage their own water resources (Iyer 2001b).

But other responses to the slogan 'get the price right` in the context of water are possible. In a classic case of correct diagnosis being followed by incorrect prescription, it does not necessarily follow that the only, and the most effective, way to conserve water and increase irrigation efficiency is to increase prices to reflect the scarcity value of water. As suggested by some scholars, there are two broad reasons for reaching this conclusion. First, raising the prices of canal water to the point where it significantly affects water demand will negatively impact farm revenues in the short and medium terms, and, moreover, such a policy will be politically indefensible. Low price increases, on the other hand, will have minimal impact on water demand. More importantly, the choice of water-inefficient crops cannot be squarely laid at the door of low water prices of canal water. Farm-level inefficiencies are not the most significant inefficiencies on existing systems of canals; the inefficiencies lie at the higher levels of the system. A better mechanism can be to enforce simple allocation rules (such as a per hectare ration) that can immediately signal the scarcity value of water without raising prices. This is politically a far more feasible step than raising prices of canal water significantly, as quantitative restrictions over water use are already a part of the management of most Indian canal systems. A transparent and equitable quota system can also free up water to be transferred to urban usage or to other farmers or to meet environmental needs. This is not to argue that one should not 'get the price right`. Till mechanisms for effective price signals are in place, 'getting the price right` is not automatically the best possible way under most circumstances in India to deal with the inefficiencies in irrigation water allocation (Ray 2005).

## CONFLICTS, CONSTITUTIONAL PROVISIONS AND INSTITUTIONS

Apart from 'getting the price right`, 'water wars` is another strand around which contemporary narratives surrounding water are being framed. Despite the increasingly audible international rhetoric surrounding 'water wars`, the incidence of violence surrounding water is mostly at the sub-national level. These conflicts can be between sectors, as is the case with the farmers` protests surrounding the transfer of water to non-agriculture use from the Hirakud reservoir in the east Indian state of Odisha; between different states, as is the case of the dispute surrounding the waters of the Cauvery River between the states of Karnataka and Tamil Nadu; or involve governments and non-governmental actors, as is the case with the struggle of the Narmada Bachao Andolan (NBA) that has been fighting against the Sardar Sarovar Project (SSP) on the Narmada River focusing on the problems of resettlement and rehabilitation. Most of the conflicts seem to be clustered around large projects and on interstate rivers.

### Conflict Resolution

With regard to interstate river disputes, Article 262 of the Constitution and the Inter-State Water Disputes Act (ISWD Act) 1956 provide the adjudication system as a mechanism for conflict resolution. This Act needs to be properly implemented by reducing delays at every stage. In addition to making the adjudication process better, it is equally important to provide an enabling environment for conflict resolution through negotiation. Institutional means should be provided for achieving this, and river basin organisations (RBOs) can perhaps fulfil this role. Conflicts between states are only one of the many types of conflicts that arise surrounding water, and there needs to be an enabling legal, institutional and policy environment to be able to deal with all these various types of conflicts effectively. Such mechanisms are sadly lacking now.

In a policy environment increasingly suffused by neoliberal prescriptions, a system of clearly defined water rights is proposed to help reduce and resolve water conflicts. This is a simplistic view as this prescription does not take into account the already existing set of claims and rights over water; in fact, the very attempts at enforcing such rights might lead to further conflicts. The set of conflicts between the people and the state needs to be looked at carefully (Iyer 2001b).

### Constitutional Mechanisms

The most important entry in the Constitution of India about water is Entry 17 in the State List that deals with water supplies, irrigation, canals, embankments, water storage and hydropower. This entry is subject to the provisions of Entry 56 of the Union List of the Constitution that primarily deals with interstate rivers and gives sweeping powers to the central government to regulate and develop interstate rivers in 'public interest`. But the centre has not been able to make any substantial use of the enabling provisions of this entry. The Eleventh and Twelfth Schedules to the Constitution list drinking water, water management, watershed development and sanitation to be devolved to panchayats and urban municipal bodies. These bodies will have an important role to play in the future, and future legislation will need to take their existence into account (Iyer 2003).

### Institutional Reforms

The National Water Resources Council (NWRC) set up by the Government of India, an important body in the Indian water sector, has no statutory backing and therefore lacks teeth. Whether giving the NWRC statutory backing will improve matters of federal water governance is a difficult question to answer. One long-standing institutional innovation that is yet to be implemented is that of the RBOs. Despite the hostility of the states to RBOs, these need to be set up on an urgent basis as water management at the level of the basin as a whole can go a long way in diffusing tensions between various stakeholders and in reducing the intensity of the conflicts. The Inter-State Council, a recommendatory body established by Presidential Order on the 28th of May 1990, is another institution which can be of use to settle disputes surrounding the waters of interstate rivers (Iyer 2003).

## WATER AND EQUITY

As the preceding discussion shows, the Indian Constitution primarily frames the debates surrounding water through spatial metaphors and statist provisions. The provisions of the Constitution look at potential conflicts primarily as between the various actors of the state. Its neglect of the social aspects of water usage is, however, not unique. Even academic work on social issues surrounding water have, more often than not, focused on issues of efficiency, that is, primarily around issues of cost recovery of irrigation water and the social reasons for non-sustainability of water usage. Issues surrounding equity have started receiving some attention of late.

The discussion that follows focuses on only two axes surrounding which issues of equity can be raised, the first one being that of gender and the second ethnicity, that is, of tribals. There are many other axes on which such analyses can take place. This discussion is merely indicative of the potential of such an exercise.

### Women and Water

In international public policy concerns surrounding water, women rarely figured in the 1950s and 1960s. By the 1970s and 1980s, it came to be recognised that women had a pivotal role to play in domestic water provisioning. They were identified as important users of water as a resource, and their role in the broader context of managing water as an environmental resource also started being recognised. During the 1980s (the UN Development Decade that focused on water), the focus on women in the context of water management was mostly to make the systems more efficient economically and did not overtly factor in gender-related concerns. In the 1990s, with the Washington Consensus firmly in place, water came to be increasingly seen as an economic good and women`s roles as water managers came to be foregrounded. More recently, it is the discourse of poverty alleviation and empowerment that frames discussions surrounding gender and water (Wallace and Coles 2005).

In the context of these changing policy orientations, it must be affirmed that in most poor rural and urban communities, it is the women and girls who have the responsibility of collecting water for domestic needs. Water collection chores do not affect all women equally because women are not one homogeneous group–the socio-economic status of the household, age and marital status, seclusion and household composition affect women`s water-related activities. Till very recently, government departments and non-governmental organisations (NGOs) focused on the provision of drinking water and for all practical purposes ignored the issues of sanitation and wastewater disposal. Lack of accessible sanitation has significant gender impacts: women bear the cost of lack of proper sanitation facilities more than men do, and they have relatively less command over financial resources to make their needs for sanitation felt in households and communities. The importance of women for the water sector and of the water sector for women is not limited to domestic water and sanitation alone. In India, women work as agricultural labourers and farmers (either as legal owners of farmland but mostly as de facto household heads). Women are the invisible backbone of Indian agriculture, and a significant proportion of the workforce engaged in agricultural labour comprises women. Even when women are actively engaged in managing farms, they are generally not recognised as 'farmers`. More often than not, their water rights are dependent on male landowners as water rights in India are tied to land rights, and land rights in the country are primarily vested with men. There is an urgent need to articulate women`s right to land and water through legal and policy changes (Kulkarni et al. 2007).

It must be evident from the foregoing discussion that water use amongst women happens along multiple axes, and they play an important role in using this resource for sustaining the household economy. If this role of women is recognised, it can go a long way in promoting more efficient and productive use of water in strengthening rural livelihoods. There is work to show that access of women to water for the purposes of production can help strengthen the livelihood condition of families by increasing their incomes; it can also aid gender empowerment in a significant manner by strengthening the bargaining positions of women (Upadhyay 2005).

### Scheduled Tribes and Water

Various surveys conducted in the tribal areas of peninsular India reveal that tribal farmers in the tribal-dominated districts earn much less income from their land compared to non-tribals in the same area. Both investments and returns on these investments by them are lower compared to non-tribals in the same area.

Water resource development in India has traditionally been an engineering-led, statist project and has not been suitable for tribal people as they usually live and work in the uplands. The explosive growth of groundwater irrigation in recent times has also bypassed them. In planning water-related interventions in tribal areas, there is a need to be sensitive to factors such as agro-climatic conditions, local topography, level of local infrastructure development and the socio-cultural characteristics of communities. Water-related interventions should also have a labour component involving 'Food for Work` programmes. Carefully implemented and sustainable water-related initiatives in these areas can help reduce the deprivation amongst tribals and enhance national food security. This can also contribute towards sustainable and more efficient utilisation of our land and water resources (Phansalkar and Verma 2004).

It must also be kept in mind that not only have the benefits of traditional water resource development projects bypassed tribals but also they have borne most of the social costs of these projects. Therefore, any new water resource development project should pass scrutiny in terms of benchmarks of ensuring the rights of tribals over land and water.

India lacks suitable legal frameworks and institutional mechanisms to manage the water sector efficiently and equitably. Irrigation is the biggest consumer of water and is the reason for most conflicts surrounding it. One of the major issues in irrigation is the low efficiency of water usage that stands at around 30–40 per cent in the case of canal irrigation systems. This needs to be urgently addressed. The conventional approach has been to lay the blame at the door of farmers and the low cost of irrigation water that apparently leads to wastages. A big part of the wastage in irrigation water happens at the supra-farm level; increasing prices will not help us to deal with this. This is not to say that pricing is not an issue; it is. But pricing reforms can only be part of a larger process that addresses broader structural and institutional concerns.

Benefits from major canal irrigation systems and most of the subsidies on irrigation water tend to go to the landed sections of rural areas. Major policy changes are needed to put social equity in the irrigation sector at the centre of our concerns. One of the initiatives in such a context can be to ensure that all the farmers growing the same crop should share equal opportunities and have equal costs. In practical terms, this means that if a farmer grows rice he must pay the same amount for the water he receives regardless of whether he is a part of a canal system or is withdrawing water from underground aquifers. Another mechanism can be to share benefits in the sense of exchangeable rights over water rather than actual water per se. Groundwater irrigation can be made more sustainable by moving from a system of free or cheap electricity for farmers to a system of minimum and exchangeable electricity quotas for every inhabitant of rural areas beyond which market rates will be charged.

Full cost recovery at the unit level in all urban centres drawing water from beyond a certain specified radius (say 5–10 kms) should be made compulsory. Water charges can be made directly proportional to the property taxes paid, and the poor can be cross-subsidised at the cost of the bigger and richer users of water in urban areas (Gujja and Shaik 2005).

The thinking on water is currently dominated by the water

resource development paradigm that essentially tries to meet demand projections made into the future by big projects for storing or transferring water. As already detailed, there are many problems with such an approach. As our discussion of the newly emerging approaches to water management shows, one cannot wholeheartedly embrace the 'alternatives` also. The thinking in the water sector is now dominated by a dichotomous approach—differences between state versus market, market versus communities, prices versus quota and small versus large systems dominate the approach. Such a dichotomous approach needs to change; the need of the hour is context-specific thinking that takes into account all the factors in a given situation.

Large-scale storage projects are, more often than not, a bad idea, especially if they are not fully integrated into extant small systems starting from the planning stage itself. Ecological sustainability should be a guiding factor in all our considerations of water planning; water is not a resource such as coal or oil; it is vital for the existence of life itself. Both supply-side and demand-side solutions are needed, and the right mix has to depend on the context. More often than, demand-side management seems to be a better option than supply-side interventions. Recognition of community rights of usage is necessary to aid efficient and equitable water management practices.

Although efficiency, both technical and economic, has to be addressed as a primary issue of public policy surrounding water, equity has to be at the centre of all water-related interventions. There is a strong case to be made for dissociating water rights and land rights. The landless must receive proportionately larger shares of rights over water to offset existing inequities in terms of land distribution. The powers of the *gram sabha* over land and water resources in the Fifth Schedule areas should be enhanced, and their already existing powers should be respected. This can go some way in ensuring that the state does not violate the rights of Scheduled Tribes in these areas. Water is essential to life, and this makes water equity central to all discourses surrounding equity in this country. Perhaps one should mention here that equity and justice are not matters of policy prescriptions; they are also matters of struggle. In this context, popular struggles matter as much as policy and legal changes; thus conflicts need not always be problematised.

## REFERENCES

Bandyopadhyay, J. and Shama Perveen. 2004. 'Interlinking of Rivers in India: Assessing the Justifications`, *Economic and Political Weekly*, 39(50): 5307–5316.

Batchelor, C., M. R. Rama and M. Rao. 2003. 'Watershed Development: A Solution to Water Shortages in Semi-arid India or Part of the Problem?`, *Land Use and Water Resources Research*, 3: 1–10.

Bhaduri, A. and Arvind Kejriwal. 2005. 'Urban Water Supply: Reforming the Reformers`, *Economic and Political Weekly*, 40(53): 5543–5545.

EPW Editorial. 2007. 'Groundwater: Half-Solutions to Groundwater Depletion`, *Economic and Political Weekly*, 42(40): 4019–4020.

Gujja, Biksham and Hajara Shaik. 2005. 'A Decade for Action: Water for Life. When Will India Cover the "Uncovered"?`, *Economic and Political Weekly*, 40(12): 1086–1089.

Hanumantha Rao, C. H. 2002. 'Sustainable Use of Water for Irrigation in Indian Agriculture`, *Economic and Political Weekly*, 37(18): 1742–1745.

———. 2000. 'Watershed Development in India: Recent Experience and Emerging Issues`, *Economic and Political Weekly*, 35(45): 3942–3947.

Iyer, R. R. 2003. *Water: Perspectives, Issues, Concerns*. New Delhi, Thousand Oaks and London: Sage Publications.

———. 2001a. 'Water: Charting a Course for the Future, Part I`, *Economic and Political Weekly*, 36(13): 1115–1122.

———. 2001b. 'Water: Charting a Course for the Future, Part II`, *Economic and Political Weekly*, 36(14 & 15): 1235–1245.

Jain, B. K., B. H. Farmer, H. Rush, H. W. West, J. A. Allan, B. Dasgupta and W. H. Boon. 1977. 'India: Underground Water Resources [and Discussion]`, *Philosophical Transactions of the Royal Society of London. Series B, Biological Sciences*, 278(962): 507–524.

Janakarajan, S. and Marcus Moench. 2006. 'Are Wells a Potential Threat to Farmers` Well-Being? Case of Deteriorating Groundwater Irrigation in Tamil Nadu`, *Economic and Political Weekly*, 41(37): 3977–3987.

Kattelmann, Richard. 1987. 'Uncertainty in Assessing Himalayan Water Resources`, *Mountain Research and Development*, 7(3): 279–286.

Kulkarni, Seema, Sara Ahmed, Swarnalata Arya, K. J. Joy and Suhas Paranjape. 2007. *Women, Water and Livelihoods*. Pune: Women and Water Network and Society for Promoting Participative Ecosystem Management (SOPPECOM).

Mehta, Lyla. 2000. 'Drought Diagnosis: Dryland Blindness of Planners`, *Economic and Political Weekly*, 35(27): 2439–2445.

Mohanty, N. and Shreekant Gupta. 2002. *Breaking the Gridlock in Water Reforms through Water Markets: International Experience and Implementation Issues for India*, Working Paper Series, Julian L. Simon Centre for Policy Research, Liberty Institute.

Palanisami, K. 2006. 'Sustainable Management of Tank Irrigation Systems in India`, *Journal of Developments in Sustainable Agriculture*, 1(1): 34–40.

Phansalkar, S. J. and Shilpa Verma. 2004. 'Water and Livelihoods: Improved Water Control as Strategy for Enhancing Tribal Livelihoods`, *Economic and Political Weekly*, 39(31): 3469–3476.

Ramachandraiah, C. 2001. 'Drinking Water as a Fundamental Right`, *Economic and Political Weekly*, 36(8): 619–621.

Ray, Isha. 2005. 'Get the Price Right: Water Prices and Irrigation Efficiency`, *Economic and Political Weekly*, 40(33): 3659–3668.

Sakthivadivel, R., P. S. Gomathinayagam and Tushaar Shah. 2004. 'Rejuvenating Irrigation Tanks through Local Institutions`, *Economic and Political Weekly*, 39(31): 3521–3526.

Shah, Tushaar. 2004. 'Water and Welfare: Critical Issues in India`s Water Future`, *Economic and Political Weekly*, 39(12): 1211–1213.

Shah, Tushaar and Barbara van Koppen. 2006. 'Is India Ripe for Integrated Water Resources Management? Fitting Water Policy to National Development Context`, *Economic and Political Weekly*, 41(31): 3413–3421.

Tejwani, K. G. 1987. 'The Himalaya-Ganges Problem`, *Mountain Research and Development*, 7(3): 323–327.

Turton, Cathryn. 2000. *Enhancing Livelihoods through Participatory Watershed Development in India*, Working Paper 131, Overseas Development Institute.

Upadhyay, Bhawana. 2005. 'Gendered Livelihoods and Multiple Water Use in North Gujarat`, *Agriculture and Human Values*, 22: 411–420.

Wallace, Tina and Anne Coles. 2005. 'Gender, Water and Development: An Introduction`, in Anne Coles and Tina Wallace (eds), *Gender, Water and Development*. Oxford and New York: Berg.

2

# LOCATING TRANSBOUNDARY WATER SHARING IN INDIA

*N. Shantha Mohan*

The sharing of rivers across political boundaries is an area of both contention and conflict, be it at the international, national, regional or local levels. Conflicts over water have steadily increased in number due to various reasons: population growth, rapid industrialisation, consumerism, pollution, environmental degradation, inequities in access to and use of water, poor governance and complications arising out of managing multiple uses across multiple users. The intensity of these conflicts has also increased in contexts where water has been a scarce commodity and a diminishing resource. The increasing pressures on the existing availability of water have created a 'crisis of unprecedented proportions` (Barker et al. 2000).

India is the largest country in South Asia, the second largest country in the world in terms of population and the seventh largest country in terms of its geographical area. It has an area of 3,287,590 sq. kms, and its population stands at 1,210,854,977, according to the 2011 census. India has one of the largest arable areas in the world with 183.95 million hectares (ha) or about 56 per cent of the total geographical area under cultivation. Agriculture contributes about 22 per cent of the gross domestic product (GDP) and employs around 65 per cent of the labour force.

India has a monsoonal climate with the southwestern monsoon in summer and the northeastern monsoon in winter contributing 70–95 per cent of the annual rainfall. The average rainfall for the whole country stands at 1,170 mm, with considerable spatial variation. The annual rainfall is uneven and varies from lower than 150 mm per year in the deserts of northwestern Rajasthan to more than 10,000 mm per year of rainfall on the Khasi Hills in the northeast. Further, most of the country receives rain for only 100 hours in a year and half of that total in less than about 20 hours (Agarwal et al. 1999).

Monsoonal rainfall and snowmelt Himalayan glaciers in the summer months are the two main sources of water in India. The rivers of India can be grouped under four categories: the Himalayan rivers, the rivers of the Deccan plateau, the coastal rivers on the west coast and the rivers of the inland drainage basin in western Rajasthan. Of these, only the Himalayan rivers are perennial and account for most of the surface water flows of the country. These include Indus, Ganga and Brahmaputra. Other rivers in peninsular India such as Narmada, Godavari, Krishna and Cauvery are completely dependent on the rains. All major rivers including Indus, Ganga, Brahmaputra, Narmada,

Mahanadi, Godavari, Krishna and Cauvery are interstate rivers insofar as they originate in one state and flow through another state or states before reaching the sea. Several smaller rivers in the country are also interstate rivers (Wood 2007).

According to the National Commission on Integrated Water Resources Development Plan (NCIWRDP 1999), the total available surface water resources in India is estimated at 1,953 billion cubic metres (BCM), out of which only 690 BCM is utilisable. The available and utilisable groundwater resources are put at 432 BCM and 396 BCM respectively. The country`s total requirement of surface and ground water by 2050 is estimated at a high and low of 1,180 BCM and 970 BCM respectively.

## COOPERATION OVER TRANSBOUNDARY RIVERS

### The International Experience

The sharing of river waters across political boundaries is a matter of conflict in many countries. Each of the 264 largest rivers in the world flow through basins that are shared by more than one nation and are home to at least 40 per cent of the world`s population (Wolf 1998). 'Water` and 'war` are two topics being talked about together with increasing frequency. The basic understanding of 'water wars` is that water is an essential resource and the scarcity of water in an arid and semi-arid environment leads to intense political pressures, often referred to as 'water stress`. Although water wars might be mythical, the connection between water and political conflicts is very real. Most water-related conflict and violence happens at the sub-national level between various social groups, between various water-use sectors or between various administrative units. While no water wars have occurred, there have been occasional instances when the lack of adequate freshwater has led to intense political instability, and even violence, on a small scale. What this means is that the geographic and political scale and the intensity of conflict are inversely related with each other (Wolf 1998). It has been observed that the absence of proper dispute resolution mechanisms can lead to 'water wars`. A close examination of the case studies cited in such literature shows that there has never been a single war fought over water alone (Wolf 1998).

The history of water dispute resolution, in contrast to that of conflict, is much more impressive. Over 3,600 treaties have been signed historically over different aspects of international waters, out of which almost 150 have been signed in the last century that deal specifically with water. These cooperative regimes are also very resilient over time, even when the riparian units are otherwise hostile to each other.

Examples of transboundary water sharing from around the world reveal that various institutional mechanisms in the form of committees, councils, commissions and regulatory boards have been established to facilitate sharing of waters and conflict resolution through cooperative and coordinated approaches.

Some of the notable examples in international cooperation in river basin water sharing are the Lower Mekong River Basin and the Nile. Both the basins have created institutional spaces that promote the member nations to coordinate and contribute to regional water resource development in spite of environmental, political and economic constraints and tensions surrounding the basin.

The reasons for their success in promoting cooperation have been that their efforts have been essentially to build confidence amongst the member countries at practical levels by focusing on common interests on small-scale programmes in terms of interventions and studies, generation of integrated basin-level databases including geographical (data from maps and satellite pictures), hydro-meteorological and socio-economic data. This is especially important since most information on the basins is either unavailable or inadequate.

An example of cooperation in the context of interstate transboundary water sharing in a federal system is the Murray-Darling River Basin in Australia. Responding to the crisis of serious conflicts amongst the states, innovative reforms were made, institutionalising the Ministerial Council and the Basin Commission. While the Commission addressed matters related to technology and administration, and the Ministerial Council addressed those related to policy. Though the decisions by these institutions are not legally binding, due to the consensual approach adopted by them, they enjoy a certain degree of political legitimacy.

### The Experience in India

India has many rivers that traverse international and interstate boundaries as well as face conflicts on common water resources. The Indus Water Treaty between India and Pakistan is an example of a successful resolution of a transboundary river water dispute. The resolution was possible on the premise that the entire Indus Basin is a single unit with sufficient water to meet the demand of both countries, and negotiations were based on a sound technical rather than a political perspective. The final award of the treaty allocated nearly 80 per cent of the water of the entire Indus system to Pakistan and 20 per cent to India. Despite criticism, the treaty has survived for nearly five decades and three wars between the countries and remains an example of successful transboundary water sharing in a politically volatile region.

The long-standing dispute between India and Bangladesh over the waters of the Ganges and the Farakka barrage was addressed when a thirty-year treaty was signed between the two countries. The treaty is a step forward towards a satisfying solution to water sharing acceptable to both countries. However, it did not include matters relating to management, conservation and prevention of pollution of their common rivers. Apart from being considered as a water sharing agreement, it is also a framework treaty as it lays down the principles for future agreements on other transboundary rivers between them.

India has a significant number of cases of interstate transboundary water sharing based on the principle of cooperation as well. These include the rivers Sutlej, Ravi, Beas, Tungabhadra, Chambal, Gandak, Parambikulam, Aliyar, Subarnareka and Jamni. Even in a complex multi-basin and multipurpose (irrigation, hydropower, domestic and industrial water supply) project as in Parambikulam–Aliyar, the establishment of a Joint Water Regulation Board comprising members from the riparian states and the cooperative approach adopted to facilitate mutual benefit have been successful. However, currently many of these cooperative arrangements for interstate water sharing face serious situations of conflict. These examples describe the importance of integrated and cooperative approaches to river basin planning, development and management. They emphasise the need to establish institutional mechanisms that promote participation of member nations and states in generating a basin-level database, conducting joint studies and evolving policies and interventions for mutual benefit.

## WATER USE AND WATER INSTITUTIONS IN THE INDIAN CONTEXT

Water as a resource has multilayered competing demands and contending uses. Agriculture is by far the biggest user of water, followed by industrial and domestic use. Irrigation supports nearly 60 per cent of agricultural production, although irrigated lands are only a third of the total arable land. The extension of irrigation has also helped to extend crop diversification. Despite growing productivity and intensity of cultivation, the irrigated crop yields are still relatively low compared to other developing countries. This is a result of poor water management.

The ultimate irrigation potential of the country according to the definitions adopted by Government of India stands at 113.5 million ha, out of which 58.5 million ha is supposed to be created from major and medium irrigation schemes and 55 million ha for minor schemes. In 1993, the area equipped for irrigation was around 50 million ha. Irrigation is mainly concentrated in the northern states of the country with the irrigated lands being fed from the perennial rivers of the Indus and Ganges river systems. The average overall water-use efficiency in canal irrigation systems is estimated at 35–40 per cent (NCIWRDP 1999). A major problem plaguing large surface irrigation systems in India is the lack of proper drainage facilities that results in salination and water logging. Various estimates point to the fact that around 6 million ha of irrigated land, around 10 per cent, of the net irrigated land in India is affected by either salinity or water logging.

There has been an explosive growth of groundwater irrigation during the latter half of the twentieth century. Irrigation from groundwater sources is found to be more than 50 per cent in most Indian states. While there has been considerable development in addressing issues regarding sharing of surface waters, it is lacking in the case of groundwater sources. It is increasingly becoming an area of stress and conflict. There seems to be a consensus that groundwater should be subject to the same rules as surface water as they belong to a single hydrological cycle, yet it remains an issue of contention.

Water to meet basic human needs, particularly 'water for life`, is of paramount importance to enhance the quality of life. The basic water requirement has been estimated at 50 litres per capita per day (lpcd) which includes water for drinking, sanitation, cooking and bathing (Gleick 1996). In rural and urban water supply, the tendency is to project future needs on the basis of per capita norms which are fairly high: 140 lpcd in urban areas and 70 lpcd in rural areas (Iyer 2007). A projected estimate of 200 lpcd and 150 lpcd in urban and rural areas respectively has been suggested by the NCIWRDP, while a common norm of 100 lpcd is regarded as adequate for both urban and rural areas (Iyer 2007).

The quality of water is as important as the quantity of water available and accessible to competing users. The primary uses considered are parameters that relate to adequate and safe drinking water, water for livelihood, water for the health of ecosystems and water free from pollution.

Under the Constitution of India (apart from the important subject of interstate rivers), water is the responsibility of states, and they are responsible for the planning, implementation and management of water-related projects. The apex body for the planning and management of water resources in the country is the Union Ministry of Water Resources (MoWR). Central organisations concerned with the water sector such as the Central Water Commission (CWC), the Central Groundwater Board and the National Water Development Agency are under the MoWR. Their mandate is to provide technical support, whereas inputs in terms of research and training are the mandate of organisations such as Water and Land Management Institutes, various agricultural universities and institutions, etc. Other central agencies having a stake in the water sector include the ministries of economic affairs, agriculture and rural development, environment and forests, housing and urban development, and health.

There have been conscious attempts to create organisations to foster interstate and centre–state coordination in the water sector. These include river boards having the responsibility of coordinating water allocation of important interstate rivers, the National Water Resources Council (NWRC) and the National Water Board (NWB). The NWRC (set up in 1983) is the apex body in the water sector in India. It is chaired by the prime minister and has the union minister of water resources and the chief ministers and lieutenant governors of all states and union territories as its members. The NWB (set up in 1990) is generally seen as the executive branch of NWRC. It is chaired by the secretary of the MoWR, and has the chief secretaries of the states and union territories, and the secretaries of the relevant union ministries and the chairman of CWC as its members. Local government bodies such as municipalities and panchayats are important institutions in the water sector on account of their mandated role in ensuring drinking water supply. Pollution control boards that generally operate under the Ministry of Environment and Forests (at both the central and the state levels) are responsible for water quality.

## RULES AND MECHANISMS TO ADDRESS TRANSBOUNDARY WATER SHARING

### The International Experience

Before making an attempt to evolve mechanisms to resolve disputes surrounding the waters of interstate rivers, it might be instructive to explore the reasons for the genesis of such disputes. Most conflicts over river waters develop surrounding large water resource development projects as more often than not they involve substantial changes to the status quo in terms of water usage patterns that have evolved over generations, and they tend to ignore the issues surrounding political power and equity. Therefore, there is an urgent need to rethink the paradigm of water resource development in the country.

River water sharing and conflict resolution between states by evolving a workable compromise are constrained by inadequate information and database, ineffective institutional mechanisms, hardened regional identities and loyalties, and threat of economic hardship. The political boundaries that divide states, which are political constructs, often subsume issues that are humane, common and social in nature. Many of the problems are due to the fact that there is an absence of a set of acceptable parameters and indicators that can form the basis of conflict resolution around issues of transboundary water sharing. While it is not possible to proclaim absolute parameters uniformly for all states and river basins, it is possible to identify those that are non-negotiable and can be applied in all cases along with river basin–specific parameters. The uniqueness of each basin and its riparian states suggests that any universal set of principles must, by necessity, be fairly general (Wolf 1998).

The Helsinki Rules (ILC 1996) and the UN Convention of 1997 provide the principles of equitable and reasonable sharing for beneficial uses as the basis for sharing transboundary river waters. Further, there is the acceptance of the principle of no 'substantial` or 'significant` harm being caused to the lower riparian by the upper riparian. The UN Convention, however, limits its rules to transboundary contexts. The Helsinki Rules and the UN Convention define reasonable and equitable use based on a non-exhaustive list of seven relevant factors. Article 6 of the International Law Commission (ILC) suggests that 'the weight to be given to each factor is to be determined by its importance` and 'all relevant factors are to be considered together`. However, Article 10 states that 'in the event of a conflict between uses ... [it shall be resolved] with special regard being given to the requirements of vital human needs`. While the Helsinki Rules deal with issues concerning pollution, navigation and timber floating, the UN Convention fails to integrate the environmental and relevant human rights concerns.

Expanding the scope of the Helsinki Rules and the UN Convention, the Berlin Rules on Water Resources enumerate five general principles that apply to states in the management of all waters. These include participatory water management, conjunctive management, integrated management, sustainability and minimisation of environmental harm. Additionally, it posits three further rules relating to water in a transboundary context. They are cooperation, equitable utilisation and avoidance of transboundary harm (Dellapenna 1997). The most cooperative of neighbouring states have found it difficult to achieve mutually acceptable arrangements to govern transboundary surface waters even in relatively humid regions where fresh water is usually sufficient to satisfy most or all needs (McCaffrey 2001). Within federal unions and at the sub-national level, states have engaged in political and legal struggles over the surface waters they share and have contended its allocation. To address these struggles, there is a need for cooperative measures with the participation of all parties concerned. In fact, evidence suggests that cooperative approaches to water scarcity problems are more likely to result in positive solutions than conflicts.

In the context of the framework provided by the guiding principles, the most important and non-negotiable parameters include water for life in terms of adequate and safe drinking water, water for livelihoods, and water for environment protection and quality of water.

### The Indian Experience

Water conflicts can be of many kinds depending on the contesting parties and the nature of the contestation. One of the many types of conflicts can be intersectoral. The resolution of these kinds of conflicts can be located in the general framework created by water-use prioritisation as specified in the National Water Policy and as implied in the Constitution of India. For the resolution of conflicts, negotiated agreements for water resource development and sharing were often the institutional arrangements resorted to. But often, there were difficulties in reaching settlements through negotiations between the parties concerned, and other mechanisms were adopted.

Conflicts surrounding river water sharing raise questions related to Indian federalism. The problems relating to conflict resolution are compounded by the lack of clear legal and institutional mechanisms available at the national level. Irrigation still accounts for more than four-fifths of all water consumption and is listed under the State List in the Indian Constitution. The most important entry regarding water is Entry 17 in the State List subject to the provisions of Entry 56 of the Union List that gives extensive powers to the central government to legislate regarding interstate rivers. However, not much use has been made of the enabling provisions provided. With the growing complexity of problems related to centre–state relations, a few consultative bodies were set up to review the policy and other related matters and to arrive at a consensus on different contentious issues. Therefore, water is as much a central subject as it is a state subject. Article 262 of the Constitution of India provides for a strong role of the centre in the adjudication of disputes surrounding interstate rivers. This article has been operationalised by the Inter-State Water Disputes Act (ISWD) 1956 that provides for the setting up of tribunals for settling disputes related to interstate rivers.

The ISWD Act states that a state government that has a water dispute with another state government may request the central government to refer the dispute to a tribunal for adjudication. The tribunal consists of a chairman and two other members nominated by the chief justice of India, from among persons who, at the time of nomination are, judges of the Supreme Court. The tribunal can appoint assessors to advise on the proceedings, investigate the matter and prepare its report along with its decision. The decision is to be published and is final and binding on the parties. The awards of the tribunals set up for Krishna, Godavari and Narmada rivers are considered as relatively successful examples of dispute resolution under this Act. But recently, there seem to be problems surrounding the success of the tribunals set up under the Act to settle disputes. The Ravi–Beas case and the Cauvery dispute are illustrative as both the awards have run into political rough weather, and the process of adjudication itself has been marked by intense politicking.

The recent amendments to the ISWD Act give the Tribunal's award the status of a decree of the Supreme Court. Yet, in some matters, the disputes remain unresolved. Though the River Boards Act (RBA) provides for arbitration as an instrument of dispute resolution, governments have resorted to adjudication, resulting in the overuse of the ISWD Act, which has led to wastage of time and resources of the nation as a whole (Gosain and Singh 2004). Disputes generally take a lot of time to reach a final settlement, though the Act amended in 2002 provides for a six-year time limit, which is a long period of time to resolve issues of such magnitude and import. Since there is an increasing tendency to avoid compliance of awards of tribunal and court orders, there is a need for greater involvement of the union government, keeping in view national interest and protection of human rights. Interstate water disputes have been a major irritant in the maintenance of cordial relations between the riparian and non-riparian states. According to the theory of community interest, a river passing through several states is one unit and maximum utilisation of its waters should be made to secure integrated development, which, however, requires mutual agreement between the states concerned.

Arbitration and negotiations are a better way to resolve disputes rather than adjudication, which should be resorted to only in the case of failure of negotiations between the disputing parties. One such institutional arrangement at the basin and sub-basin levels is the river basin organisation (RBO) under the centrally legislated River Boards Act 1956, which was legislated under the provisions of Article 56 of the Union List. The RBOs regulate and develop interstate rivers and river valleys on the request of the riparian state. The board has members with expertise in various fields such as irrigation, engineering, flood control, water and soil conservation, administration and finance, thus allowing for a holistic approach to the arbitration process. However, no such river board has been established, largely because no state government was in favour of such a course (Iyer 2007).

Governance relating to water is further decentralised through the Eleventh and Twelfth Schedules to the Constitution, which lay down lists of subjects to be devolved to panchayats and *nagar palikas*. The List includes drinking water, water management, watershed development and sanitation. These local self-government bodies that have an important role to play in relation to water distribution in an equitable and efficient manner need to be rejuvenated. However, there are very few institutions at the middle level to resolve conflicts. For example, if disputes arise between communities within a river basin or canal system, there are very few, if any, mechanisms for resolving them in a satisfactory and participatory manner. Water bureaucracies at this level remain inaccessible. Institutional innovations at the basin or sub-basin level can play an important and useful role in promoting conflict resolution by facilitating the representation and participation of all water users in the community.

Assessing the inadequacy of the existing mechanisms to address conflicts between states, the Administrative Reforms Commission, the Rajamannar Committee and the Sarkaria Commission recommended the setting up of an Inter-State Council (ISC) as envisaged under Article 263 of the Constitution with the responsibility to inquire into and advise upon disputes between states. The ISC was set up in 1990 as a federating consultative body under the chairmanship of the prime minister. The Council consists of chief ministers of all states and union territories as well as six union ministers of cabinet rank. It is a recommendatory body that investigates and deliberates such subjects, in which some or all states or the union and one or more states have a common interest, and makes recommendations upon any such subject for the better coordination of policy and action (Iyer 2002).

Given the complexities of water use within society, developing, allocating and managing it equitably and efficiently and ensuring environmental sustainability requires that disparate voices are heard and respected in decisions over common waters and use of scarce financial and human resources. At the micro level, there are several non-official efforts that have been suggested by civil society to address issues of transboundary water sharing, which need to be strengthened. One such example is that of the initiative undertaken by the Madras Institute of Development Studies to create a platform for dialogue for farmers of the two contending riparian states of Karnataka and Tamil Nadu in the Cauvery Basin. Though it is a multi-stakeholder platform, it is primarily a dialogue for farmers, resulting in the establishment of the 'Cauvery Family`. The members of this family have developed empathy and understanding for each other`s problems and needs and are therefore able to influence their respective governments from the collective stakeholder perspective.

Another example is the initiative of Gomukh in Maharashtra, a non-governmental organisation involved in interventions related to land and water issues in the Bhima Basin. The Kolwan Valley experience highlights the need to bring together all stakeholders—communities, state agencies and civil society organisations—to find solutions to critical water-sharing problems. Negotiation has been an important element in the decision-making process. To facilitate informed negotiation positions, networks and coalitions among stakeholders have been established and strengthened.

In both the cases discussed, accommodation of different stakeholder interests is central to the decision-making process. It allows for an inclusive framework (institutional and administrative) within which people with different interests can discuss the polarised discourse on water (Rogers and Hall 2003). Further, it encourages a consensual framework that accommodates and appreciates different stakeholder interests and points of view including the concerns of equity and sustainability. If such a consensual framework is not evolved, 'rivers will continue to divide us, emotionally and politically, leading to a million revolts` (Gujja et al. 2006). The approach also emphasises the importance of generating reliable data arising out of a common interest and a shared vision of developing the basin concerned, honouring each other`s requests for information, dialogue and transparent procedures to participate in the negotiation processes to resolve conflicts. 'Stakeholder representatives must get formally involved in the sharing of agreements at the basin scale. This will allow the negotiations to "deepen" and the agreements to be more effectively implemented and enforced` (Vaz and Zaag 2003).

An analysis of the mechanisms adopted by the state and civil society highlights both strengths and limitations in addressing issues related to interstate water sharing and conflict resolution. Interstate water-sharing disputes occur when the water sharing cuts across political boundaries, cultural identities and livelihoods. Under the circumstances, it appears that the ISC is the only unexplored mechanism that has the potential to develop into an effective institutional mechanism by establishing various subject-specific fora for sustained consultations. However, the existing structure and governance has to be expanded to make these forums inclusive, participative and consultative so that the interests of all stakeholders, such as the government, academics, policymakers, media, civil society organisations, legal experts and water users, is integrated. For this, the IWRM has emerged as a logical concept as an alternative to the sectoral, top–down management approach to deal with problems surrounding water. It facilitates an interdisciplinary, multidisciplinary, intersectoral and multi-stakeholder approach to integrate different perspectives in promoting equitable water distribution and conflict resolution among various users.

## REFERENCES

Agarwal, Anil, Sunita Narain and Srabani Sen (eds). 1999. *The State of India's Environment: The Citizen's Fifth Report*, No. 5. New Delhi: Centre for Science and Environment.

Barker, Rudolf, Barbara van Koppen and Tushar Shah. 2000. *A Global Perspective on Water Scarcity/Poverty: Achievements and Challenges for Water Resources Management*. Colombo: International Water Management Institute.

Cauvery Water Disputes Tribunal. 2007. *The Report of the Cauvery Water Disputes Tribunal with the Decision*, Vol. III. New Delhi.

Dellapenna, Joseph W. Villanova. 1997. *The Berlin Rules on Water Resources: The New Paradigm for International Water Law*. University School of Law.

Gleick, P. H., 1996. 'Basic Water Requirements for Human Activities: Meeting Basic Needs', *Water International*, 21(2): 83–92.

Gosain A. K. and K. Singh. 2004. 'Water Rights in Indian Transboundary Watercourses`, *Jalvigyan Sameeksha*, 19(1–2): 51–60.

Gujja, Biksham, K. J. Joy, Suhas Paranjape, Vinod Goud and Shruti Vispute. 2006. '"Million Revolts" in the Making`, *Economic and Political Weekly*, 41(7): 18–24.

International Law Commission (ILC). 1996. *Helsinki Rules on the Uses of the Waters of International Rivers*. London.

Iyer, Ramaswamy R. 2007. *Towards Water Wisdom: Limits, Justice, Harmony*. New Delhi: Sage Publications.

———. 2002. 'Inter-State Water Disputes Act 1956 Difficulties and Solutions`, *Economic and Political Weekly,* 13 July: 2907–2910.

McCaffrey, S.C. 2001. 'International Water Law for the 21st Century: The Contribution of the UN Convention`, *Journal of Contemporary Water Research and Education*, 118(1): 11–19.

National Commission on Integrated Water Resources Development Plan (NCIWRDP). 1999. Report. New Delhi: Ministry of Water Resources, Government of India.

Rogers, Peter and Alan Hall. 2003. 'Effective Water Governance`, GWP Technical Committee.

United Nations. 1997. *UN Convention on the Non-Navigable Uses of International Water Courses*.

Vaz, Alvaro Carmo and Pieter van der Zaag. 2003. *Sharing the Incomati Waters: Cooperation and Competition in the Balance*. UNESCO.

Wolf, Aaron. T. 1998. 'Conflict and Cooperation along International Waterways`, *Water Policy*, 1(2): 251–65.

Wood, John R. 2007. *The Politics of Water Resource Development in India: The Narmada Dams Controversy*. New Delhi: Sage Publications.

3

# WATER AS AN ETHIC

## Three Ways of Talking about Water and Rights[1]

*Sailen Routray and N. Shantha Mohan*

We remember growing up in social milieus in which regular access to water was not guaranteed. Till a generation ago, growing up in small towns and villages in India meant that even playing with water was a taboo. If a drop of water got spilt on the floor or on the dining table and a child started drawing something with it, immediately she would be admonished by an elder, especially by the grandparents. This was because a folk belief that said playing with water resulted in droughts was still strong. The need to conserve water was deeply embedded in the strictures and taboos that governed everyday life.

The links between water and what constitutes ethical social practice in India go very deep. In many of the Puranas,[2] one of the ways in which the gods punish wayward kings who do not follow the dharma is by visiting droughts upon the kingdoms they ruled. The corollary to such narratives was the fact that all rulers and kings could hope to increase their powers in the material world and earn merit for the other world by constructing water bodies.

For example, David Mosse discusses the ways in which in the creation of water bodies in Ramnad district in Tamil Nadu, exercises of political power and notions of ethical practice all fed into each other for centuries all together. The creation of tanks was supposed to accrue merit to the rulers of the region. But the creation of such water bodies extended land under paddy cultivation in the area and increased its human population as well (Mosse 2003).

Even now when the rise of the developmental state has significantly eroded the autonomy of communities, it is not unusual to come across instances of people constructing and maintaining communal water bodies because of the merit that is supposed to accrue to one from such charitable acts. Merit accrued to people if they created public water bodies. There were strictures against polluting water bodies as well. These were also a matter of taboos–urinating, defecating or polluting rivers and tanks were forbidden and were seen as reprehensible acts.

But the past in India is not completely unproblematic. Water was also a site where caste differences and differentiation were built. The relationship between various jati groups was mediated through the ritual and symbolic values of water. Generally speaking, in most regions of India, jatis have apparently been ranked according to a gradation imposed by water. Generally speaking (and this is a huge generalisation), a person belonging to a jati that was less powerful and esteemed could and will accept water from the hands of someone belonging to a more powerful and esteemed jati and not vice versa. Similarly, food cooked in ghee or oil could be eaten by anyone no matter what its source was. But the acceptance of food cooked in water was subject to strictures similar to the strictures governing that of acceptance of water. Thus, water played, and many would argue continues to play, an important role in the reproduction of social roles and institutions in India.

But it can be argued that this way of acting upon the world is no longer available to us. Moreover, these ways of acting upon the world, specifically with respect to water, might even be in contradiction with the constitutional morality that purports to govern our actions in post-independence republican India. Increasingly, access to key resources in India is framed through the discourse of rights, this being true for a resource like water as well. In this, the discussions in India also reflect the international narratives surrounding water rights.

## WATER RIGHTS

Increasingly, discussions surrounding water and rights have three important strands. The first one has to do with property. This discussion, primarily of an economic and public policy persuasion, sees water as an economic good and views property rights as one way of ensuring proper transactions related to water. The second strand of discussions happens around rights of states over water, and the 'water wars` discourse dominated this for a while. The third strand of discussions occurs around the 'human right` to water and the ways in which entitlements to minimum levels of water can be ensured to all, especially the poor and the underprivileged. In some sense, one can see at play the perceived dominance of three sets of socio-political actors in these three strands: the first strand privileges 'the market` and corporations; the second strand foregrounds statist concerns and tends to legitimise the state as the actor par excellence in the water sector; the third strand foregrounds 'people`.

### Property Rights over Water

According to the UN agencies, water gained recognition as an economic good after the declaration of the Dublin Principles in 1992. A large part of the discussion surrounding water and property rights have been around seeing water as an economic good, getting the price right for promoting efficiency and the sustainability of water usage. The discussions on property rights and water in India have been about pricing and cost recovery (Rogers et al. 2002). This discussion has had two foci: water for irrigation and urban drinking water.

Treating water as a public good and its management, especially that of irrigation water by state agencies, is seen to lead to inefficient usages of water. Market-based mechanisms are seen as an alternative. There are two broad sets of reasons that are given for preferring water markets to administered pricing. Treating water as a public good and the consequent administrative delivery has the danger of being captured by interest groups. These administrative bodies are also perceived to be inefficient. The critiques of free-market solutions argue that water markets need significant regulation. Moreover, private property rights over water need enforcement by the government. The need for such enforcement creates problems similar to those involved in treating water as a public good and the consequent administrated pricing and delivery. Moreover, water markets fail regularly. The introduction of private property rights over water and the consequent market mechanisms do not automatically guarantee efficiency. Market-based mechanisms also do not always take into account issues surrounding water equity (Routray 2010).

Recently, there have been a few cases in India where urban municipal bodies have tried to privatise water distribution in cities. The proposed changes to bring in market-based mechanisms in the water sector (in the case of both irrigation water and urban drinking water provisioning) are seen as part of a broader neoliberal trend in governance in India. As Priya Sangameswaran (2009) observes in the case of Maharashtra, urban drinking water, rural drinking water and irrigation water have been increasingly subjected to a greater drive towards private-sector participation, which changes the discourse of water provisioning by depoliticising the imperatives and practices of governmental organisations. The neoliberal goal of self-sufficiency is proposed as a desirable goal, without taking into account whether in a sector such as water (especially urban drinking water) this is feasible or desirable (ibid. 2009).

We are not arguing that there is no need to 'get the price right` in every instance. In fact, the way in which water usage is charged for in the cases of urban drinking water and irrigation water tends to benefit rich farmers and urban middle class and upper-middle class citizens the most. The concerns of the poor and the vulnerable are rarely part of the policy discourse. The rich and the relatively better off need not be subsidised. But rationalisation of subsidies does not need to translate into either fixing property rights over water or merely 'getting the price right'. In times of growing agrarian distress and rapid expansion of the urban population in India, using arguments of inefficiency of governmental provisioning of water to push for privatisation of water can only be termed as misguided.

### States' Rights over Water

The international conventions, rules and declarations that frame discussions surrounding rights and water, not unpredictably, foreground states as the legitimate social actors in the sectors concerned. These deal with rivers that flow through more than one country. The Helsinki Rules and the UN Convention of 1997 are important in this regard as these provide the principles of sharing transboundary river waters. The Helsinki Rules deal with issues such as pollution, navigation and timber floating. But the UN Convention of 1997 does not deal with environmental and relevant human rights concerns in an integrated fashion. With respect to transboundary river waters, upper riparian states often claim absolute territorial sovereignty and control over the water within their borders, with scant regard of effects on downstream states. Downstream states tend to make claims about the absolute integrity of the watercourses and demand the non-disturbance of the quantity and quality of water flowing from the upstream states. The Helsinki Rules provide the principle of 'equitable utilisation' that recognises the right of riparian states of usage of water from common sources if they do not interfere unreasonably with the usage by other riparian states. It must be evident that the Helsinki Rules treat international transboundary rivers and their drainage basins as indivisible hydrologic units, which are expected to be managed as a single unit (Mohan 2010).

The Berlin Rules on Water Resources expands the scope of the Helsinki Rules and the UN Convention of 1997. The former enumerates five principles applying to the states–participatory, conjunctive and integrated management, sustainability and the minimisation of harm to the environment. The Berlin Rules also posit three additional rules related to water sharing in an international transboundary context: cooperation, equitable utilisation and avoidance of harm. As evident from this discussion, states do not have absolute rights over the waters of transboundary water bodies (Mohan 2010).

Water is listed under Entry 17 under the State List in the Constitution of India. This entry is subjected to the provisions of Entry 56 of the Union List. The latter entry gives the central government powers to legislate on matters related to interstate rivers, but it has not been used to the fullest possible extent. Further Article 262 of the Constitution provides adjudicatory function to the centre in conflicts related to interstate rivers. The Inter-State Water Disputes Act (ISWD Act), 1956 that provides for the formation of tribunals for settling transboundary river disputes was promulgated under this Article (Mohan and Routray 2011).

### Water as a Human Right

The preceding discussion showed that the international principles, rules and frameworks for water governance as well as the Indian Constitution frame issues surrounding water through a statist optic. This neglect of the social aspects of water usage is definitely not unique to these. Academic work on social issues related to water has generally dealt with issues of efficiency and sustainability. Comparatively speaking, less attention has been given to issues surrounding equity (Routray 2010).

In this regard, there is an increasing move to argue for a human right to water that tries to take into account these concerns of equity. Scholars argue that from an individual`s perspective, there are clear advantages to having human rights over water. The social benefits of recognising such a right are perceived to be significant. The question is whether such a human right to water should be a right subordinate to other human rights such as right to health and right to life (as recognised by the international bill on human rights) or whether it should have an independent recognition. In either case, institution of a human right to water will have far-reaching consequences. There are difficulties associated with the fragmentation of the right to water. Thus the Committee on Economic, Cultural and Social Rights of the United Nations Economic and Social Council (ECOSOC) has taken a non-fragmented and holistic approach in order to ensure the required water supplies to realise the rights under the International Covenant on Economic, Social and Cultural Rights (ICESCR). This can be seen from the ECOSOC`s General Comment 15 in November 2002, which recognised the right to water as an independent human right. This comment is non-binding and does not spell out the obligations of states to ensure the human right to water. But it is significant as it provides the basis for an independent human right to water (Bluemel 2005).

A human right to water would entail obligations to respect, protect and fulfil. This will involve ensuring access to water with a specified quantity and quality in a non-discriminatory fashion. Ensuring water rights might be difficult because attempts at ensuring one community`s rights might violate another`s, for instance, as is the case with big dams. There are further choices to be made between the right to water and the right to development since industry is amongst the biggest polluters of fresh water sources and cleaning up pollution by shutting down, relocating or adapting to cleaner technologies will have developmental costs. From the perspective of the states, such an approach is seen to put constraints over adequate cost recovery. These costs are perceived as not only financial but also legal, cultural and institutional. These costs will vary according to socio-economic, cultural and political contexts of specific countries. South Africa has already enshrined the human right to water as a part of its constitution and has started taking steps to ensure the enjoyment of such a right by its citizens. Argentina also has an explicitly stated right to water in its constitution and has taken steps within its court system to protect this right (Bluemel 2005).

In India, a quantum of 150 lpcd and 200 lpcd of water has been proposed by the NCIWRDP as adequate for rural and urban areas respectively, while a common norm of 100 lpcd is seen as sufficient for both (Iyer 2007). In India`s Constitution, the right to water is not stated explicitly, but this right is implicit in the constitutional right to life that has been interpreted by Indian courts to include a right to clean and sufficient water. The right to water has been derived by the courts in India from Article 21 of the Constitution that provides for the right to life. The right to water in India has evolved through judicial interpretation and not through legislative action. This is evident in the judgments being passed by the court in cases such as *Narmada Bachao Andolan v. Union of India*, *M.C. Mehta v. Union of India* and *A.P. Pollution Control Board v. Prof. M.V. Nayadu*. In these cases, the Supreme Court has passed injunctions upholding the state`s duty not to pollute water resources, to prevent potential pollution of drinking water during industrial development, to improve the sewage system and to provide clean drinking water to all its citizens. The Indian Supreme Court has also declared groundwater to be a public asset (Narain 2010)

Questions surrounding water rights in India are also issues about access. In large parts of rural India, caste-based barriers to accessing water, especially drinking water, are still prevalent. There are laws that try to deal with this situation, for example, s.3 (xiii) of the Scheduled Castes and Scheduled Tribes (Prevention of Atrocities) Act, 1989 deals with problems of access to water and makes it a punishable offence for persons belonging to non-Scheduled Tribe (ST)/Scheduled Caste (SC) communities to either obstruct usage of sources of water by SCs and STs or to spoil such sources of water. It must be mentioned in this regard that traditional managers of water bodies in the commons (such as tanks), especially in peninsular India, often belonged to SC communities. But irrigation laws in Andhra Pradesh and Tamil Nadu do not acknowledge the roles of such traditional water managers and their rights. With regard to other uses of water such as traditional fisher folk, the changed policies of the state often affect them adversely. As this shows, governmental policies are often inconsistent with the constitutionally given and judicially interpreted right to water. The need to adequately operationalise such a right stems from not only constitutional and juridical imperatives but also international imperatives such as the Millennium Development Goals and the obligations under General Comment No. 15 (Muralidhar 2006).

## WATER AS AN ETHIC

In contrast to seeing water as a right, we posit that there is a need to frame discussions surrounding water and equity in terms of an ethic. Water as a resource itself comprises an ethic. Unlike other 'static' resources such as land and minerals, water is dynamic. Water is also renewable, a characteristic which makes the physical exercise of a 'right'—in the sense of excluding other potential users—difficult. Because as a resource, water can be used multiple times for multiple usages, it can lend itself as much as a site for conflict as for cooperation.

In this regard, instead of figuring out details of what will be the legal, economic and institutional repercussions of constituting water as a right, we list here a few principles that may help in taking the discussion on water, equity and rights forward. These are based on the understanding that duties and rights are intertwined—every right, as we learnt as students in school, has a corresponding duty. The peculiar nature of water makes the fulfilment of these duties imperative. Water is essential for life and is the basis for obtaining other capabilities such as food and health that are necessary for human well-being. Hence, debates surrounding water and equity have to go beyond the narrow and legalistic calculation of rights and duties to a discussion of water as an ethic.

The first principle that has to be kept in mind while discussing water and equity and therefore water as an ethic is that of ideological pragmatism. As seen in the earlier sections of this essay, discussions surrounding water and rights are often framed around ideological positions that seem to foreground states, markets or communities as custodians par excellence of water as a resource. One needs to get away from this kind of ideological polarisation with respect to water. In some instances such as densely populated urban areas, provisioning by governmental organisations might make sense, whereas facilitation of community provisioning of drinking water supplies might be more relevant in thinly populated rural areas. Major subsidisation of the domestic water usage of poor urban citizens might be necessary, whereas rich rural farmers undertaking cash crop cultivation might deserve minor subsidy support.

The second principle to be kept in mind is that of subsidiarity. If water can be provisioned at a lower scale of administration or community, then that should be encouraged. This also means that the responsibility is on organisations at a higher level to follow rules such as 'no harm to the resource`. The third principle is a Gandhian one–it is the principle of *antyodaya* (roughly translated it means putting the last, or the weakest, at the first). With respect to water, in practice, it will mean that in the event of any conflict with respect to claims or access to water as a resource, the claims and concerns of the weaker party in a dispute should be foregrounded.

The fourth principle that has to frame discussions surrounding water is the indivisibility of water as a resource and the way it can work as an integrative device in thinking about issues surrounding development and equity. Current processes of development violate the 'bodies` of sources of freshwater such as rivers, tanks and lakes with impunity. Socio-economic planning and its implementation take place in India as if water and water bodies are incidental to such a process. Especially with respect to urban water resources, city planning has to take place as if water mattered. It will help us think and act about issues of inequity in other resources such as land and forests in a much more integrated fashion.

### Steps to be Taken

If we see water as an ethic, then one cannot merely hand out a set of prescriptions that are not context specific. But certain broad directions in which things need to start moving soon can be indicated. One needs to identify a minimum quantum of water (for drinking, cooking, sanitation and health) that is an entitlement of every person on account of being a citizen of India. For obvious reasons, this will need to be minimally defined, and governmental agencies responsible for ensuring supply and access of this water will need to be identified. Instead of targeting the vulnerable, the attempt should be to ensure universal access to this quantum of water. A code also needs to be developed for governmental organisations to deal with the pollution of fresh water sources. Similarly, corporate liability will need to be defined, banning usages of certain types of common resources of surface water and groundwater. A place has to be created for civil society organisations so that they can act as catalysts for desirable change for ensuring the right to water, for watching over the activities of government organisations and corporations, and for playing a pedagogic role with respect to the wider public (Muralidhar 2006).

There was an older ethic of water that governed the usage of the resource in India, informed by a certain understanding of dharma. Under the constitutional morality that is supposed to guide resource use in postcolonial India, that ethic is not available to us any longer. The discourse that is available to us is one of rights. As we saw in this essay, there are three important ways of thinking about water and rights in the world as well as in India. First, private property rights over water and issues surrounding cost recovery; second, rights of states over water according to international laws and conventions and the possibilities of cooperation and conflict between states based on these rights; and third, around the human right to water. This essay is most comfortable with the third way of talking about rights. While recognising a human right to water, it is necessary to start thinking about water in new ways. Thinking about water as an ethic and about the principles that can govern such an ethic might be one such way in which we can perhaps start thinking about water, equity and rights productively.

## NOTES

1. This title is structured in a fashion similar to a book by Vijay Nambisan titled *Language as an Ethic*.

2. This also applies to histories that are hybrid narratives of genealogies, stories and historical events around people, places, deities and lineages.

## REFERENCES

Bluemel, E. B. 2005. 'The Implications of Formulating a Human Right to Water`, *Ecology Law Quarterly*, 31: 957–1006.

Iyer, Ramaswamy R. 2007. *Towards Water Wisdom: Limits, Justice, Harmony*. New Delhi: Sage Publications.

Mohan, Shantha N. 2010. 'Locating Transboundary Water Sharing in India`, in N. Shantha Mohan, Sailen Routray and N. Shashikumar (eds), *River Water Sharing: Transboundary Conflict and Cooperation in India,* pp. 3–22. New Delhi: Routledge.

Mohan, Shantha N. and Sailen Routray. 2011. 'Resolving Inter-state Water Sharing Disputes`, *Seminar*, 626: 31–35.

Mosse, D. 2003. *The Rule of Water: Statecraft, Ecology and Collective Action in South India*. Oxford: Oxford University Press.

Muralidhar, S. 2006. 'The Right to Water: An Overview of the Indian Legal Regime', in Eibe Riedel and Peter Rothen (eds), *The Human Right to Water*, pp. 65–81. Berlin: Berliner Wissenschafts-Verlag.

Nambisan, Vijay. 2003. *Language as an Ethic*. New Delhi: Penguin Books.

Narain, V. 2010. 'Water as a Fundamental Right: A Perspective from India', *Vermont Law Review*, 34(4): 917–925.

Rogers, P., R. de Silva and R. Bhatia. 2002. 'Water is an Economic Good: How to Use Prices to Promote Equity, Efficiency, and Sustainability', *Water Policy*, 4: 1–17.

Routray, S. 2010. 'The Water Sector in India: An Overview', in N. Shantha Mohan, Sailen Routray and N. Shashikumar (eds), *River Water Sharing: Transboundary Conflict and Cooperation in India*, pp. 23–44. New Delhi: Routledge.

Sangameswaran, P. 2009. 'Neoliberalism and Water Reforms in Western India: Commercialization, Self-Sufficiency, and Regulatory Bodies', *Geoforum*, 40: 228–238.

4

# SECURING LIVELIHOODS

## Emergence of the 'Social' in a Watershed Project in Odisha

*Sailen Routray and N. Shantha Mohan*

With the traditional water resource development paradigm being contested, watershed development is increasingly seen as an important strategy for the development of marginal areas wherein rain-fed agriculture is prevalent. Critiques of the fact that traditional watershed development approaches are iniquitous and favour the landed and elite sections of rural areas have led to the growth of the watershed-plus approach. A key aspect of the watershed-plus approach as opposed to the traditional watershed development approaches is the importance given to livelihoods.

The watershed-plus approach and its focus on livelihoods and user groups as delivery mechanisms for projects (and the use of such mechanisms for ensuring 'participation') is often seen as part of a depoliticising process that purportedly subverts the functioning of multipurpose local government (Baviskar 2004, Manor 2004). Thus, the assessment of such a process has often been a normative one. In this essay, we try and offer a narrative with a slightly different focus. Instead of judging whether the new generation watershed-plus projects do indeed deliver on the promises of livelihood generation for marginalised communities and whether they are effective or equitable, we try to shift the narrative into a perceptual and descriptive domain. What we try and do is map out the consequences of such a change in the focus of watershed projects in the ways in which beneficiaries and lower-level staff perceive these. We also try and elaborate the effects that such changes have with respect to the ways in which certain social processes operate on the ground and the modes in which people perceive the government and its apparatus.

We do this by drawing upon fieldwork undertaken in the project area of an ongoing watershed-plus project–the Western Odisha Rural Livelihood Project (WORLP)[1]–in Kalahandi district in southwestern Odisha, which is being implemented under the aegis of the Odisha Watershed Development Mission (OWDM). We posit that one of the important results of this process of refocusing on livelihoods has been the growth of the 'social' as a site and tool of governmental action. The emergence of the 'social' through the refocusing on livelihoods is reflected in the organisational structure and project priorities of WORLP as well as the perceptions of the project staff working at various levels of the project. By doing this, we sidestep the issues surrounding 'depoliticisation' and offer a slightly different account of the processes set in motion on the ground by focusing on livelihoods in the case of a specific new-generation watershed-plus project. Thus, the overall thrust of this essay is empirical in nature.

## WATERSHED DEVELOPMENT IN INDIA

In order to be able to better contextualise the recent changes in the approaches in watershed development, we trace a brief history of relevant processes and events here. During the colonial period, watershed development initiatives consisted of preventing soil erosion in the catchments of river valley projects and other programmes for conserving soil and moisture. These initiatives lacked a holistic approach towards watershed development (Samra and Sharma 2009). The period immediately after independence was marked by the dominance of the water resource development paradigm, which was characterised by the building of big dams and multipurpose river valley projects (Klingensmith 2007). Over the last three decades, the canal-oriented, water resources development framework based on big dams for meeting the irrigation, water and livelihood needs of the country has been increasingly critiqued by social scientists and those involved with social movements (Dhawan 1989, Singh 1990). Commentators in India have suggested that the watershed approach could function as an alternative to mitigate the adverse effects of the water resources development approach (Mehta 2000, 2005).

Since the 1970s, there has been a growing interest in watershed development and other localised and decentralised ways of resource usage and management. The Rural Works Programme (RWP) launched in 1970–71, which had watershed-related components, can be seen as a precursor to the Drought Prone

Area Programme (DPAP), which is, in many ways, the mother of all watershed development programmes in India. During the mid-term appraisal of the Fourth Five Year Plan, the RWP was redesigned as the DPAP (GoI 1994). Many commentators also trace the roots of modern watershed development projects in India to purportedly successful village-level projects of the 1970s, of which the most talked about ones are Sukhomajri in Haryana and Ralegaon Siddhi in Maharashtra (Kerr 2002).

Following the publication of the Report of the National Commission on Agriculture in 1974, the Desert Development Programme (DDP) was started in 1977–78 (GoI 1994). During the period covering the 1970s and the early 1980s, the performance of watershed programmes was measured mainly through indicators with a biophysical focus such as soil loss and water tables (Turton 2000). The Swaminathan Committee Report of 1982 reemphasised the ecological goals of watershed development programmes and recommended schemes that had a component of community participation (GoI 1994). In 1987, the DPAP was reorganised around water harvesting. The late 1980s saw a change in priorities, with the focus shifting from measuring progress only through improvements in natural resources to the more overtly social concerns such as ensuring livelihoods and broadening participation (Turton 2000).

During the early 1990s, the Union Ministry of Rural Development (MoRD) became the nodal ministry for watershed development in India, after which one of its chief initiatives was the issuing of, what was called, 'Common Guidelines for Watershed Development` in 1994. Apart from other objectives such as an increase in agricultural productivity and employment, regeneration of village commons and checking migration, these guidelines also promoted a 'community-based' approach. This was part of a larger push towards participatory watershed management in India in which many important non-governmental organisations (NGOs) such as MYRADA (Mysore Resettlement and Development Agency) and donor agencies such as the UK Government's Department for International Development (DFID) played an important role by emphasising the new participatory watershed development approaches that focus on livelihoods and poverty alleviation (Chhotray 2007).

In the year 2000, the Ministry of Agriculture (MoA) revised the guidelines for the National Watershed Development Project for Rainfed Areas (NWDPRA), following the overall thrust on participation, equity and sustainability. The guidelines issued by the MoA were named as 'WARASA (Watershed Areas' Rainfed Agricultural Systems Approach)-Jan Sahbhagita Guidelines'. Following this, the MoRD revised the Common Guidelines in 2001 and then again in April 2003, which were then called the Hariyali Guidelines. Since the implementation of these changes, watershed development has become central to the process of governmental interventions in rural development with its focus on livelihoods and poverty alleviation (GoI 2006).

The shifting of focus from biophysical regeneration to livelihoods and poverty reduction has seen the emergence of the 'social' as a site and trope of governmental intervention as opposed to the technical and the scientific. The implications of such a change of focus need to be understood. This is done by drawing upon fieldwork undertaken in an ongoing participatory watershed development project–WORLP–that has an explicit livelihood focus, in one of the most 'backward' districts of the country, Kalahandi, in the state of Odisha. Kalahandi is infamous in India as the land of hunger and starvation deaths. The district is seen as being beset with droughts and water-stress. It is also overwhelmingly a rural district with a high incidence of poverty. The initiation of livelihood programmes based on the sustainable usage of local natural resources has been advocated as a developmental intervention that can meet the needs of the district (Pradhan 1993). In this context, the district is a productive site for studying the operation of a new-generation, livelihood-focused, watershed-plus project such as WORLP.

## THE SITE AND THE FIELD

### The Area and the People

Kalahandi is perceived to be one of the most backward districts in India. It is part of a broader region in the southwest part of the state of Odisha called the KBK region (taking the initials of the undivided districts of Kalahandi, Bolangir and Koraput), which is characterised by widespread poverty, lack of healthcare and other public services, and low levels of attainment in terms of socio-economic indicators (Dash 2007). The economy of the district is primarily agricultural in nature, with minimal industrial activity seen here (Pati 2001). It was a princely state that was incorporated into the state of Odisha after independence. The area of the district is 7,920 sq. kms, and it has a population of around 1,573,054 according to the 2011 Census.

Tribal groups comprise a major proportion of the population of the district, with their share at around 29 per cent of the total, whereas the other numerically significant demographic group, that of the Scheduled Castes (SCs), comprises around 17 per cent of the population (Banik 2007). The district has become synonymous with hunger in India because of frequent reports of starvation deaths there (Currie 2000). Kalahandi is generally seen as a drought-prone region, which is perceived to be resulting in resource degradation and the concomitant erosion of livelihood opportunities. Politics in the state and the region have focused on the logistics of elections rather than tackling the issues of deprivation, and many development programmes have been launched there without taking into account the basic underlying causes of poverty and deprivation (Mohanty 1998).

### The Western Orissa Rural Livelihood Project

Increasingly, watershed development, especially the livelihood-plus approach, is seen as an appropriate developmental intervention in areas perceived as marginal drylands such as Kalahandi. WORLP, a watershed project operational in Kalahandi and promoted by the Government of Odisha (GoO) and DFID, followed a watershed-plus approach. Apart from Kalahandi, it was operational in three other districts of western Odisha–Nuapada, Bolangir and Bargarh.

The project was managed by the OWDM, which is an autonomous agency under the control of the Department of Agriculture of the GoO. At the district level, the District Watershed Mission (DWM), Kalahandi, managed the project, with the project director as the head, who was assisted by assistant project directors (APDs) and capacity building team (CBT) members. At the sub-district level, project implementing agencies (PIAs) were involved in the project at the level of the blocks. WORLP was operational in six blocks in Kalahandi with three PIAs being NGOs and the other three being managed directly by the government. The project team at the level of the PIA has watershed development team (WDT) members and livelihood support team (LST) members. One of the WDT members is in charge of the 'social` aspects of the project and is primarily involved in managing the 'plus` aspects of the project`s activities.

Each PIA has the responsibility for around ten village-level watershed development committees (henceforth called committees), which at the most primary level of the project are responsible for the execution of the watershed development work. These committees have been registered legally as societies, and each has a president, a secretary and committee members. Each committee is supposed to have four community link workers (CLWs) to assist its work, with one of the CLW posts being that of the CLW social.

Before the commencement of the actual project activities, the households in the project villages were divided into four categories—very poor, poor, manageable and well off. On the basis of these categories, the households were assigned numbers and colour codes. The project has four broad heads under which activities take place—administration, community development, natural resource management (NRM), and the watershed-plus component comprising a revolving fund (RF) and grant. In the last category of project activities, self-help groups (SHGs) of women got loans at zero per cent interest for livelihood-generation activities. Grants ranging from Rs 4,000 to Rs 7,000 were supposed to be given to only those households that fall under the 'very poor` and 'poor` categories in order to help them enhance their livelihood options.

## DEVELOPMENT THROUGH LIVELIHOOD ENHANCEMENT: NEW SITES OF GOVERNMENTAL INTERVENTION

### Implications of the Focus on Livelihoods

In many ways, the current focus on livelihoods in watershed development has turned matters through a full circle. When programmes such as DDP and DPAP were started, they had a broader mandate of rural development. In the 1980s, with increasing criticism surrounding the ineffectiveness of the programmes and the lack of observable results in terms of biophysical criteria, and following the recommendations of the Hanumantha Rao Committee, at least 75 per cent of the project amount was mandated to be spent on NRM-related activities. Following changes in the international and national policy atmosphere and governance agendas, non-NRM activities have again started gaining prominence. This has happened not through the trope of rural development but through tropes such as 'livelihoods`, 'process focus` and 'participation`, and the emergence of the 'social` as an important site of governmental intervention.

This has also happened as a result of critiques of older watershed development approaches that were seen as being inequitable and as favouring the landed, elite sections of village society (Sangameswaran 2006). The argument of this essay is as follows: by refocusing on watershed development as a livelihood-related intervention (as opposed to an intervention only or primarily focused on environmental regeneration), the 'social` has emerged as a distinct site of governmental intervention. The watershed-plus approach is not a way of 'socialising` the former technocratic approaches to watershed development but is one way (amongst many other parallel interventions) through which the state 'seeps` into village society. This 'seepage` is made possible by the practices that are operationalised through new tropes of governmental intervention.

### Emergence of Social Watershed

The watershed-plus approach is not merely about adding 'social concerns` to an already existing biophysical intervention. In Kalahandi, though the names of the micro-watersheds generally do not have the name of the village(s), the so-called micro-watershed is not a bio-geographical unit but a social unit composed of one or more villages having around 500 ha of treatable area. The units that were chosen for interventions in WORLP constituted a village or a set of villages and not micro-watersheds. The only reference to micro-watersheds seems to be in the names that the committees give to themselves. The government has identified villages that need 'watershed treatment` on the basis of certain criteria, which also include certain 'social` criteria such as the proportion of SCs and Scheduled Tribes (STs), the very poor and the poor in the population. The basic units of intervention in watershed-related treatments have thus been villages (a social unit) and not any 'biophysical` unit. Middle-level officials on deputation from the soil conservation department emphasised this fact, criticising the 'unscientific` categorisation of micro-watersheds. According to these officials, prior to the period when watershed development work started taking place under the OWDM, 'technocratic norms` for site and intervention selection prevailed, with watershed development having a strong 'technical` focus.

Earlier, the soil conservation department dealt primarily with farmers or peasants. The landless played the role of labourers and not beneficiaries. On account of the adoption of the watershed-plus approach and work undertaken through the state- and district-level watershed missions, the government apparatus now has to deal with new population groups, such as the primarily landless SC groups. These groups generally did not come into contact with the state apparatus through the soil conservation department.

Questions around livelihoods are central to the watershed-plus approach, which is premised upon the understanding that there are significant unaddressed social concerns surrounding the exclusion of the non-landed in the 'traditional` watershed projects. This changed focus on the livelihoods of hitherto marginal groups also tries to address the concerns surrounding the capture of watershed-related interventions by the landed elite.

This felt and expressed need for a 'plus` to the traditional watershed development approach presupposes that 'technical` aspects such as the building of tanks are not seen as 'social` interventions. However, the generation of livelihoods is seen as a specifically 'social concern`, which unites both 'technical` interventions such as building tanks and wells (that are put under the accounting head of NRM in WORLP) and 'social interventions` such as livelihood-related loans and grants.

This is reflected in the organisational structure and recruitment practices of OWDM, in general, and WORLP, in particular. In WORLP, the concern surrounding livelihoods has led to the creation of the LST in addition to the WDT at the level of the PIAs, whose stated job profile focuses on the promotion of livelihood-related activities. The LST members are expected to support the effective implementation of livelihood-related interventions, and their mandated roles include extending help to form women`s SHGs, to help these groups diversify their livelihood options and build federations, and to facilitate access to the various schemes of the government.

The project mandates that each LST should have four persons, with at least two of them women. This team is expected to have competencies in various social techniques such as participatory methodologies, gender analysis, monitoring and evaluation, running of micro-enterprises, and group formation, and it is supposed to facilitate the development of processes such as those of leadership development and conflict management (Johnston et al. 2002). As this job description shows, most aspects of their work are related to what can be considered as 'social` interventions, which are a part of the more 'technical` aspects of the project that deal with natural resource management. Thus, the institutionalisation of livelihood concerns inside the project design and structure of WORLP has led to its 'socialisation`.

### Vernacular Usages of the Category of Watershed

The term 'watershed` itself is understood differently by various groups of people. In Odia, the actual and literal translation of the term 'watershed` is *jala bibhajika*, but sometimes it is translated as *jalachhaya*. However, in the field, no one uses the Odia term(s) for 'watershed` at all. Everyone uses the term 'watershed` in everyday conversations in Odia, though the word means different things to different people. The dominant understanding amongst watershed staff, especially the middle and the lower level staff among WDT members and secretaries of the committees, of the term 'watershed` is that of a project. They do not talk about watersheds *per se* but about discrete projects such as WORLP or the various DPAP projects. The top-level officials of the district watershed mission use the term 'watershed` in the way it is 'supposed` to be used—as a biophysical/environmental intervention. Most villagers generally talk about 'watershed' in the same vein as they would talk about the police or the agriculture department. Thus, they do not see it as either a project or a 'mission' but as another government department, though different in terms of its orientation and functioning. However, this understanding varies across PIAs. For instance, in the NGO PIA, there are a few beneficiaries who see it as a discrete project, whereas in the case of the governmental PIA, almost everyone sees it as a government department. For example, people in villages, while referring to the money coming into the village through the 'watershed', would see it as *sarkari tanka* or government money, in the same way that they would talk about interventions by other government departments. Thus, the very meaning of the word 'watershed' is contested socially. The following section tries to trace the contours of the way in which the 'social' seems to emerge as a new site and motif of governmental action.

## THE FOCUS ON LIVELIHOODS AND THE EMERGENCE OF THE 'SOCIAL'

### The Perceived Importance of the 'Social'

It was a warm day in March, one of those days when one feels that spring in Odisha is not a concoction of the imagination of a slightly delusional poet. There was not even a nip of coolness in the air, but it was not hot either. The first author was travelling inside an old, ratty ambassador car with Mr Mahanty, a WDT member working with one of the governmental PIAs to attend a meeting of a committee. The meeting apparently could not take place the previous month due to a lack of quorum. This time, the secretary had sent an emergency notice to all the committee members to attend the meeting, and Mr Mahanty was hoping that the meeting would finally take place.

Mr Mahanty, a reticent man, spoke slowly, emphasising every word that he uttered. He was curious about the researcher and the work, and after the initial pleasantries, he looked at the researcher in amusement and said, 'Your work sounds interesting; during our student days, we could not even think that such work was possible.' After talking for some time about his M.Sc. dissertation, his interest in research and his regret at not having followed a career in research, he said, 'These days "social" is very important.' He gave the example of the watershed mission and said, 'See, at every level of the project, there is some social person; at the district level, there is a social CBT member, at the PIA level, there is a WDT social, and at the village level, there is a CLW social. Recently, they [have been] thinking about eliminating the posts of the CLW, but one hears that the post of the CLW social will remain. This is only to be expected. When I started working more than forty years ago, it was just about doing technical work and distributing stuff. Now it is all about motivating people. When we started working, we never thought that things [would] come to such a pass. Now we have to be servile to these ignorant villagers to get their own work done. Not that I mind it too much. It is after all people's work. But I am not used to this, that is all there is to it. Now for young people such as you, this new focus on social things is, of course, an opportunity.'

As mentioned earlier, this focus on the 'social' is not merely seen in the narratives that the project staff members tell each other and other curious observers. It is there in the very architecture of the project itself. As regards the way in which the accounting heads of the project work, there are heads that are generally perceived as 'technical` and others that are perceived as 'social`—NRM is seen as coming under the technical head, while RF and grant are seen as coming under the 'social` head. The money budgeted under the RF head was mandated to be given to SHGs. In fact, the tasks of the WDT social and the CLW social, along with those of some of the LSTs, were supposed to focus on the work of the SHGs and other aspects of livelihood enhancement such as ensuring that the livelihood grants were put to productive use.

### The Social as 'Messy'

The 'social`, in many accounts of work given by staff of the project, was seen as something messy. Once, in the NGO PIA, all the staff members, apart from the PIA himself and the WDT engineer, had gone on leave because of a long weekend. The work in the village of Kalampada has been stuck for quite some time, and even the committee meetings were not taking place. The secretary of the Kalampada committee had fixed the meeting at a time when the meeting of another committee was also taking place. Thus, the PIA went to attend the meeting of the other village, and sent the WDT engineer to Kalampada.

The WDT was very reluctant to go, and we left slightly late. For a change, when we arrived at the venue, which was the village school, everyone was already there including the president and the secretary. When the meeting started, it emerged that the reason for the stalemate in the work of the committee was something relatively small but symbolically big. One of the committee members, who had taken the contract as the head of a user group to construct a drain in one of the hamlets of the village (as a community development initiative through WORLP), had apparently done sub-standard work and had overcharged. The problem was that he had refused to share the spoils with anyone else. At the meeting, people almost came to blows, but the WDT did nothing to diffuse the situation. Ultimately, the relevant committee member agreed to donate a couple of thousand rupees to a temple that was being constructed in the village and agreed to give bricks for the construction of a platform around a big tree at a public place for the use of everyone.

On the way back to the office, when the WDT member was asked as to why he did not intervene in the meeting at all, he said, 'It`s beneath me to get embroiled in village politics; I am much better off dealing with estimates. Merely because the relevant staff is absent, I need not deal with all this messy social stuff.` He then gave a comparative account of the work he had done in the same block, but with a governmental PIA as an engineering WDT in another project. According to him, that project did not focus on the so-called social aspects of work that much and, therefore, the 'real` work took place in a much more efficient fashion. He gave the example of the village Laimera, where he had constructed three water harvesting structures on a single stream, and he referred to this work as a 'visible` piece of work that people still remember him for. He said, 'Ei social social hei khali jaha politics badhuchhi–au kanata labha nahele heuchhi apana mote kuhantu?` ('Only politics is increasing because of this focus on the "social". Otherwise what`s the benefit out of this, please tell me?`)

This was not an isolated case. The discomfort of the engineering staff in dealing with non-technical or social aspects of the project was much evident from the manner in which way they did not want to fill in for social WDT members when the latter were on leave. Even senior project staff members, especially some officers drawn from the soil conservation department, saw the overtly social aspects of the project as 'messy`. Often, during interviews, they would voice concerns about the deteriorating quality of the 'technical` aspects of the work because of the need to factor in what they termed as 'social concerns`. Thus, the 'social` was construed as something messy owing to the fact that it was difficult to deal with and manage, and it was seen as something that adversely affected the quality of the technical aspects of the work.

### The 'Social' as a Marker between Governmental Organisations and NGOs

Many PIAs, APDs and CBT members saw the 'social` as a distinguishing marker between governmental PIAs and NGO PIAs. Once, after a review meeting held at the district headquarters, a governmental PIA elaborated informally over lunch about the differences between how he worked and how an NGO PIA worked. He said, 'See, the NGOs are slightly better than us in terms of the work related to the social aspects of the project, and this should be acknowledged. Since they have been working in these areas for quite a few years, they also have a better understanding of social aspects of these kinds of projects. Moreover, they are used to working in a contractual fashion; therefore, they find it much easier to deal with the contractual staff of the projects hired under the District Watershed Mission [DWM]. To be honest, we governmental PIAs, who are mostly on deputation, are yet to get a hang of the ways of dealing with the contractual staff. But we are definitely better at doing the technical work. Most of these NGO PIAs, in Kalahandi as well as elsewhere, have never employed proper engineers, and these organisations have very little experience in doing construction work. So the villagers can lead them on, whereas no villager can take us for a ride. The NGOs also have better experience in these new things such as community mobilisation and awareness building. But we are also learning. After all, all this new social nonsense is not rocket science.`

Narratives surrounding the 'social` were also used as a marker to distinguish between the earlier forms of watershed-related interventions in the soil conservation department and the work now being done under the aegis of OWDM. The higher-level staff members of the DWM, Kalahandi, see this difference through the trope of participation. As a senior official commented in an interview, 'Earlier when the soil conservation department used to work on watersheds, there was no participation by the people. An engineer would go and survey the area and depending on the availability of funds and the needs of the watershed, he would draw up estimates depending on technical criteria. And only when the actual earthwork started, people would come to know that a project has come to their village. Now there is people`s participation because of decentralised planning. Therefore, the importance of the social aspects of the work has grown considerably.` This focus on the 'social` as a marker of difference posits certain aspects of the work of the project as not being 'social`. For example, the work of accounting and auditing is not seen as being 'social` but as requiring technical expertise that is difficult to acquire.

### Emergence of the 'Social' and Imbrications in the Field

The watershed-plus approach with its focus on livelihoods can be seen as a way in which watershed projects, and in our case the WORLP, is trying to 'socialise` the manner in which the government functions. For example, the way the project is structured–with all the work supposed to be carried out through the village-level micro-watershed committees–is in itself a significant move at 'socialisation`. The committee members and other village-level functionaries are not chosen on the basis of education or competence, though the secretary is expected to be at least a matriculate as he has to maintain the records of the committee. This change has meant that the 'social` is being incorporated into the machinery of the government through certain institutional assemblages such as watershed committees, SHGs and user groups.

This focus on the 'social` seen in interaction with many other processes in the field has provided some interesting results, one of which has been that the project has aided vastly increased sightings of the state. Many of the villagers identified project staff from WORLP as the most visible amongst all government departments. The creation of the watershed committees and the fact that the work took place through them meant that at least one government staff member visited the village at least once a month to attend the monthly meetings of the committees. Similarly, the work surrounding the small grants and RFs involved frequent visits by the staff of the project of both the governmental and NGO PIAs for facilitation and monitoring. Thus, one of the more important results of the focus on the 'social` has been to increase the number of sightings of government staff and thus, in effect, of the government and the state itself.

The focus on the 'social' has also led to a dramatic increase in the number of direct beneficiaries. The livelihood promotion budget, comprising the RF for the SHGs and the livelihood grants for individual households, constitutes more than a quarter of the total budgeted amounts released to the various committees under the project. The minimum amount that could be distributed as livelihood grants is Rs 4,000, though sometimes committees distributed Rs 3,000 per grant to maximise the coverage of beneficiaries. On an average, around 150 households belonging to the 'poor' and 'very poor' categories got livelihood grants in the micro-watersheds of the PIAs under study. The number of households covered under the RF component is at least 100 in most micro-watersheds. Even allowing for some overlap of households that have benefited from both the RFs and livelihood grants, this is a large number of households, considering the fact that most micro-watersheds have around 400–500 households.

In fact, the emergence of the 'social' due to a focus on livelihoods seems to be premised upon such an effect. In many ways, this phenomenon of spreading things thin and ensuring the sightings of the state functionaries seems to be built into the very project architecture. For example, one of the goals for all project staff members, especially for the staff members hired to deal with the overtly social aspects of the project, has been to ensure that at least 80 per cent of households in the project areas are covered through SHGs. The staff members sometimes resent this, as it expands the scope of their work and makes them much more 'accessible' to the villagers.

The promotion of SHGs in the project area has fed into other kinds of processes in a few cases. The emergence of the 'social' and the attendant establishment and strengthening of institutions such as SHGs have resulted in the increasing penetration of micro-credit institutions in many areas. Because of the existence of a robust network of these SHGs, micro-credit institutions have found it easy to operate in these villages. Most SHGs in the micro-watersheds in the project area of the governmental PIA have a relatively poor record of ensuring the return of the loans received through WORLP as RFs. But it would be perhaps unfruitful to judge these institutions as ineffective on these grounds. By forming these SHGs and handholding them during the initial part of their existence, the project has created institutions that have gone on to perform other, and sometimes, similar roles.

Many women stated that by being part of SHGs, they have been able to become 'forward` (confident) and that earlier, they would not have the confidence to talk to a government official and other outsiders. But now they are able to do so. They see this as a direct result of being a member of the SHGs, and thus a result of their experience of training, exposure visits to other areas and the increased opportunities of interacting with the 'outside` world within the village.

Another important aspect of the emergence of the 'social` is the importance that is given to 'process` in WORLP. The process dimensions of the social components of the work are stressed upon to a greater extent compared to the same dimensions of the 'technical` or 'engineering` aspects of the project work. This may be read as suggesting that perhaps the project managers have greater anxieties regarding the social aspects of the work. But this can be posed in another way as well. The way in which the auditors would want to ensure whether certain social goals were fulfilled or not was by insisting that certain indicators and processes of the social components of the project work were consistently followed. Consequently, a substantial part of the work took place to ensure that the auditors could be satisfied as and when auditing was carried out.

Watershed development is increasingly being seen as an alternative to the traditional paradigm of water resource development based on big dams. Simultaneously, following critiques of approaches to watershed development that emphasised biophysical criteria, concerns surrounding non-biophysical issues such as those involving livelihoods, especially in the dryland areas, have come to the forefront during the same period of time. On the basis of fieldwork undertaken in Kalahandi in the project area of WORLP, this essay has argued that the increasing importance given to livelihoods can be read as part of a process of emergence of the 'social' as a site, object and domain of governmental interventions. Such a focus on the 'social' is built into the project design as well as the actual everyday practices of the project. Most of the project staff interviewed tended to foreground the increasing importance given to social aspects (such as the formation of groups, distribution of livelihood-related grants and loans, and following proper processes while doing the work, which they saw as constituting the 'social') in the project.

Although watershed is construed as a technical biophysical category, the meaning of the term 'watershed' is socially mediated and contested. The emergence of the 'social' is seen as an important marker of difference between the work of the NGOs and government organisations, on the one hand, and between the work of the OWDM and the state soil conservation department, on the other. While the NGOs and OWDM are perceived to be better at implementing the social aspects of watershed development, government organisations and the soil conservation department are perceived to be better at overseeing the 'traditional`, technical aspects of the work.

The undertaking of new kinds of project activities related to the livelihoods of traditionally marginal communities in watershed development and the concomitant rise of the 'social` has been accompanied by the state reaching out deep into village society through organisational forms such as NGOs as project implementing agencies and the evolution of new institutions such as micro-watershed development committees at the village level. The emergence of the 'social` as a site and mode of governance has increased the sightings of the state for villagers by increasing the intensity and the variety of the ways in which governmental staff interact with them. It has also increased, to a very large extent, the total number of beneficiaries that come into contact with the governmental apparatus, cutting across NGOs and governmental organisations as implementing agencies. The breadth of such a phenomenon and its theoretical implications need to be teased out by further research.

## NOTES

1. The project was being implemented during the time of fieldwork for this paper that took place in January 2009–February 2010.

## REFERENCES


Banik, Dan. 2007. *Starvation and India's Democracy*. London and New York: Routledge.

Baviskar, A. 2004. 'Between Micro-politics and Administrative Imperatives: Decentralisation and the Watershed Mission in Madhya Pradesh, India`, *European Journal of Development Research*, 16(1): 26–40.

Chhotray, Vasudha. 2007. 'The "Anti-politics Machine" in India: Depoliticisation through Local Institution Building for Participatory Watershed Development`, *Journal of Development Studies*, 43(6): 1037–1056.

Currie, Bob. 2000. *The Politics of Hunger in India: A Study of Democracy, Governance and Kalahandi's Poverty*. Chennai: MacMillan India Ltd.

Dash, Satya Prakash. 2007. 'Development and Poverty in an Indian State: A Study of KBK Districts of Orissa`, *Social Change*, 37(2): 76–98.

Dhawan, B. D. 1989. 'Mounting Antagonism towards Big Dams`, *Economic and Political Weekly*, 24(20): 1096–1099.

Government of India (GoI). 2006. *From Hariyali to Neeranchal: Report of the Technical Committee on Watershed Programmes in India*. New Delhi: Department of Land Resources, Ministry of Rural Development, Government of India.

——. 1994. *Report of the Technical Committee on Drought-Prone Areas Programme and Desert Development Programme*. New Delhi: Ministry of Rural Development, Government of India.

Johnston, B., A. Panda and R. Ghosal. 2002. *Establishing Livelihood Support Teams*, Working Paper 2, Western Orissa Rural Livelihoods Project, Bhubaneshwar.

Kerr, John. 2002. 'Watershed Development, Environmental Services, and Poverty Alleviation in India`, *World Development*, 30(8): 1387–1400.

Klingensmith, Daniel. 2007. *One Valley and a Thousand: Dams, Nationalism, and Development*. New Delhi: Oxford University Press.

Manor, J. 2004. 'User Committees: A Potentially Damaging Second Wave of Decentralisation?`, *European Journal of Development Research*, 16(1): 192–213.

Mehta, Lyla. 2005. *The Politics and Poetics of Water: Naturalising Scarcity in Western India*. New Delhi: Orient Longman.

——. 2000. 'Drought Diagnosis: Dryland Blindness of Planners`, *Economic and Political Weekly*, 35(27): 2439–2445.

Mohanty, Manoranjan. 1998. 'Orissa Elections and Kalahandi`s Tularam`, *Economic and Political Weekly*, 33(5): 204–206.

Pati, Biswamoy. 2001. 'Tracing the Social History of a Famine: Kalahandi (1800–1992)`, in Biswamoy Pati, *Situating Social History: Orissa 1800–1997*, pp. 99–139. New Delhi: Orient Longman.

Pradhan, Jagdish. 1993. 'Drought in Kalahandi: The Real Story`, *Economic and Political Weekly*, 28(22): 1084–1088.

Samra, J. S. and K. D. Sharma. 2009. 'Watershed Development: How to Make "Invisible" Impacts "Visible"?`, *Current Science*, 96(2): 203–205.

Sangameswaran, Priya. 2006. 'Equity in Watershed Development: A Case Study in Western Maharashtra`, *Economic and Political Weekly*, 41(21): 2157–2165.

Singh, Satyajit K. 1990. 'Evaluating Large Dams in India`, *Economic and Political Weekly*, 25(11): 561–574.

Turton, Cathryn. 2000. *Enhancing Livelihoods through Participatory Watershed Development in India*, Working Paper 131, Overseas Development Institute, London.

5

# SARKAR IN THE BACKYARD

## State Fabrication in a Watershed Project in Kalahandi[1]

*Sailen Routray and N. Shantha Mohan*

It is two thirty in the afternoon of the month of *jyestha*, and one of the authors is sitting in a tiny stand-alone room with naked, non-plastered brick walls in the village of Mahulpani that houses the office of the Sanjore Micro-Watershed Development Committee, a village-level institution set up under the aegis of the Odisha Watershed Development Mission (OWDM) that implements the Western Orissa Rural Livelihoods Project (WORLP). There is a crowd of women belonging to self-help groups sitting just outside the door of the room. Inside the room, a couple of middle-level staff of the project are trying to prepare business development plans (BDPs) for dozens of largely illiterate project beneficiaries who have already taken grants and bought goats for farming. The secretary of the committee rushes into the room and tells me, 'Asun, bhauja jagichhi' ('Please come, my wife is waiting'). This is a call for having lunch at his place. But he pointedly ignores the project staff who must also be hungry, who have no other way of getting lunch in the village so late in the afternoon and who had indicated to the secretary the previous day that they would want him to make arrangements for lunch. The author feels somewhat awkward, but feeling that flight is the better part of valour, he leaves the room for lunch.

This incident from fieldwork done in Kalahandi in western Odisha raises a set of important questions. First, why did the BDPs need to be created at all after the distribution of grants when they should have been made before the event a long time back? How is it that most of the grantees have been able to buy goats when these are officially seen as 'the bane' of watershed development projects in India? How is it that a lower-level project functionary is able to defy his seniors by withdrawing even the basic courtesies of village society, such as offering food, that too in public? In short, how has the workings of government and the process of state fabrication changed by the mushrooming of missions in India over the last three decades or so?

In this essay, we deal with something related yet much smaller in scope. Based on fieldwork conducted in the site of a new-generation participatory governmental watershed-plus development project called Western Orissa Rural Livelihoods Project (WORLP) in the district of Kalahandi in western Odisha, we argue that the emergent forms of state fabrication in India associated with the establishment of missions involves the creation of new institutional assemblages that incorporate organisations and institutions earlier seen as lying outside the body of the state (such as non-governmental organisations [NGOs] and community-based organisations [CBOs]) into the body of the state.

WORLP is a Department of International Development (DFID)–funded watershed development project for livelihoods development being implemented by the Orissa Watershed Development Mission. In the district of Kalahandi, the project is being implemented by six project implementing agencies (PIAs) in six developmental blocks out of which three are NGOs. Each PIA oversees the work of ten village-level micro-watershed development committees that are societies set up under the Indian Societies Registration Act of 1860, and these committees undertake the actual work of the project in the villages. They have a president and a secretary and constitute of committee members representing the various population groups and hamlets in the villages.

Thus the creation of these village-level institutions (that are technically societies or NGOs) is one of the ways in which the state has extended and morphed itself in the ground. This helps the governmental apparatus to reach deep into hitherto marginal rural areas and population groups, with important impacts on the ground regarding the functioning of the state and the way it is experienced by people. In particular, we tease out one aspect of this morphing of the state on the ground involving increasing convergence in the workings and everyday practices of the governmental and non-governmental organisations. This convergence can be seen in terms of the profile of the staff and in the organisational culture and strategies. We argue that instead of positing additional domains of sociality such as political society, formulations such as 'state in society' might be more relevant in understanding such processes of change.

## GROWTH OF MISSIONS AND QUOTIDIAN MODES OF STATE FABRICATION

Most narratives surrounding the state in India posit decolonisation in the period 1947–52 as the phase that marked a clear shift in the working of the state and in the workings of Indian politics. In contrast to this, I argue that we can locate a major shift around the mid-1980s regarding the way in which the 'government is done' in India. Immediately after decolonisation, the state inherited a colonial administrative structure that consisted of line departments for administrative work. In this structure, development administration became another arm of the state. This continued till the 1980s, when significant changes started taking place.

We claim that till this period, state fabrication in India happened in the 'symbolic mode' in which the state remained at a distance with respect to village society despite the rapid expansion of the bureaucratic apparatus, and the state had a dominantly coercive intent. In contrast to this, the last three decades have seen state fabrication in, what we call, the 'quotidian mode', which has seen the governmental apparatus reaching deep into hitherto marginal areas and population groups. Over this period, much governmental work, such as in the sectors of health, education and watershed development, has been routed through para-statal organisations. These organisations are called missions and are often societies registered under the Indian Societies Registration Act of 1860. These operate at the level of both the state and central governments, and have a target-driven approach towards achieving policy goals within pre-set time frames.

Missions such as the various state and district Watershed Development Missions allow for new institutional assemblages based on the avowed principles of participation and decentralisation. This has also involved a growing shift from focusing on 'scientific' technologies to 'social' technologies of statecraft, for example, in the field of water resources, the shift has been from an almost exclusive focus on big dams that were feats of engineering to watershed development and innovations in 'social technology' such as watershed development committees and self-help groups. This is true of other sectors such as health and education as well where missions increasingly undertake activities that were earlier performed by government departments in addition to new kinds of programmatic and social interventions. Organisational forms traditionally seen as part of civil society (such as NGOs) are increasingly being incorporated into the ambit of the state through projectisation in the missions.

Theoretically, the most sophisticated account of such processes of multiplication of technologies of governmentality and the simultaneous morphing of the state has been those surrounding political society (Chatterjee 2006 [2004]). In this formulation, Chatterjee argues that the domain of negotiation and claim-making with the state that the various subaltern social groups engage with maps out on the terrain of political society, the domain of civil society being the preserve of rights-bearing 'citizens'.

In an article published in *Economic and Political Weekly*, Chatterjee extends this formulation by borrowing from Kalyan Sanyal's work on primitive accumulation (Chatterjee 2008). He tries to account for the proliferation of various governmental technologies (that he identifies as ameliorative) by making it a part of a broader narrative of capital in which governments try to reverse the effects of primitive accumulation by welfare programmes that support lives and livelihoods. He argues that social agents in the domain of civil society are a part of the narrative of corporate capital, whereas those in the domain of political society are part of non-corporate capital. He further posits that relatively successful contestation and claim-making by such agents has happened primarily within an urban setting (ibid.).

Such an argument has been criticised for setting up unhelpful binaries, for disguising welfare colonialism as a measure for offsetting dispossession and for characterising civil society as the domain of legality and hegemony when apparently it should be read as a domain characterised by domination (Baviskar and Sundar 2008). Doubts have also been expressed about the newness of such a formulation, the conflation of welfare intentions with outcomes, which is overtly economistic in nature (John and Deshpande 2008). It has also been pointed out that this reading of the post-1990 social change in rural India, which has an exclusive focus on class as an axis of power, is riddled with a few factual inaccuracies and glosses over the abdication of the arena of governance by the state (Shah 2008).

This formulation and its critiques reproduce a certain tendency in the social sciences in India that tend to reify the state. At the same time, there has also been a simultaneous lack of ethnographic engagement with the apparatus of the state in India. The dominant strands of scholarship on the state in India have focused on the 'nature' of the Indian state and have displaced questions surrounding the state into realm of politics. There is a need to ethnographically interrogate the actual practices of state fabrication on the ground.

Over the last two decades, the work of scholars such as James Manor, Paul Brass, Akhil Gupta, Barbara Harriss-White, Robert

Wade and Jonathan Parry has had the state itself as an object of study and analysis by focusing on the ways by which various omissions and commissions of the state play out on the ground, and the way such actions are seen, experienced and commented on by people (Fuller and Harriss 2000: 10–14). We locate our argument within this broader anthropologically oriented literature that takes the state itself as an object of study. We try and understand the morphing of the state on the ground by using ethnographic methods that interrogate the shifts in the workings of the state that have been concomitant with the incorporation of civil society organisations into the body of the state. This helps to fill in a gap in literature as similarities or differences between governmental and non-governmental organisations have generally been constructed around their effects (Kamat 2002).

We locate this work within a broadly defined 'state-in-society' approach as developed by Joel S. Migdal (2001) that sees the state as a field of power that has a paradoxical nature having the image of a clearly bounded, unified organisation, on the one hand, and of fragmentary everyday practices, on the other. Because of its focus on both practices and images, this approach allows us to focus on process rather than on outcomes. Such an approach also helps us shift the focus from Marxist ideas of hegemony or liberal ideas of consensus to the actual messiness of everyday morphings of state and society on the ground. As the state-in-society approach does not see the state as a fixed ideological entity, it helps us map out the actual morphing of the state on the ground as it comes into contact with various social forces and, in turn, accommodates different ethical orders and logics (ibid.).

## INCREASING CONVERGENCE IN EVERYDAY PRACTICE BETWEEN GOS AND NGOS

In this section, we follow a broadly defined state-in-society approach to understand the morphing of the state on the ground. In the first sub-section, we show how the growth of the mission mode of 'doing government' has led to changes in everyday practices of governmental organisations (GOs). In the two subsequent sub-sections, using the tropes of provisionalisation of the state and pluralisation of the logics of the state, we show how the incorporation of civil society organisations into the body of the state is reflected in its morphing on the ground. In the final sub-section, we bring in the experiences of villagers as they perceive and experience this convergence between GOs and NGOs.

### The Case of a Review Meeting

Within the first month or so of starting fieldwork in Kalahandi, one of the authors had occasion to attend a monthly review meeting of one of the government PIAs in the district, and accompanied the PIA from his place of residence to the office. On the day of the meeting, the PIA leaves home at around ten in the morning when the meeting itself is scheduled around ten-thirty. The PIA at this point of time is Mr Kundu.

It takes nearly 90 minutes to clear a 35 km stretch of a national highway, and the PIA's car reached the office around 11.45 am. By that time, a large number of the staff, around twenty in number, has arrived, but not everyone has reached. So the meeting does not start immediately. The mood is raucous. There are people milling around, joking, staff of the opposite sex flirting with each other and men horsing around. It comes off as something of a shock. It does not feel like the review meeting of a GO at all. It feels like the experience-sharing workshop of some middle-sized grass-roots NGO. By the time everyone arrives and the meeting starts, it is around noon. The attendance is more or less full, and there is a shortage of chairs.

This is another feature of review meetings of the watershed mission. At every meeting, there seems to be a shortage of chairs. Everyone complains about it, but no one seems to want to do anything about it. Because of the shortage of chairs, a couple of people sit on the window ledge. And the meeting then starts in earnest. First, attendance is taken in an informal manner. Two of the important project staff, a livelihood support team (LST) and a watershed development team (WDT) member, seem to be on leave from the WORLP project.

Just before the meeting starts, the PIA Mr Kundu goes out to take a call that he receives on his mobile phone. In the meantime, everyone starts talking about the strike that they had recently. Before looking at the work of the watershed mission in Kalahandi, a scoping exercise was done regarding the work of the district administration in Kalahandi towards the beginning of fieldwork. On one of the visits to the Kalahandi district collectorate, one of the authors saw a group of people sitting in a dharna (a sit-in demonstration) in front of the gate of the collector's office with its representatives giving rousing speeches. It was the district-level WDT staff agitating for better salaries and permanence of work. Later with informal interactions with the PIAs, it appeared that they sympathised with most demands of the staff; but some demands, especially the one of being made permanent, were seen as slightly unrealistic. By the time of the review meeting being discussed, the strike had been withdrawn and things had settled down. In fact, a large number of the staff had not participated in the strike. Now a large part of the conversation in the absence of Mr Kundu in the room was about whether the salaries of those who participated in the strike (and did not report for work) would be deducted or not.

One of the most surprising things was the way the lunch was conducted. Food for everyone was ordered from a restaurant close by. Those who wanted vegetarian food had to specify their order. Most people preferred and ordered non-vegetarian food. Dheeraj, one WDT member, took the responsibility of getting the meals to the office. Two of the other staff also went with him to help him. It took Dheeraj a long time to get back. By the time he returned, the meeting was about to be over and he had missed most of the meeting. The review was almost over when he reached, and with the arrival of food, everyone started getting fidgety and things were wrapped up soon.

Since there were no tables and there was a shortage of chairs, all of us sat on the ground and started eating. After ten minutes or so, the PIA and the other officer also came out of the PIA's room and started having lunch with everyone present. There was pleasant banter between the PIA and the staff; he was pleasantly needling those who had participated in the strike. The latter were ribbing him about getting paid for the days on which they had struck work on the grounds that after the strike, they had worked overtime and had achieved the targets for the month.

There was little of the overall symbolism of hierarchy that supposedly operates in most government organisations. The PIA had got the same meal packet as everyone else, and he also joined the others in having food sitting on the floor when he could easily have had food in his room on the table. The preceding description indicates a convergence of the organisational cultures of GOs and NGOs, with GOs increasingly adopting the organisational culture of how NGOs are supposed to function.

### Provisionalisation of the State

Although states are as contingent as any other social artifact, the myth of the state is generally sustained by a certain imperative to portray itself as a permanent entity that lies above society. The state is seen as an agent of change but not necessarily as a temporal artifact. In most small towns and cities in India, the state is made visible and available to the population by its material body, primarily offices. In most small cities and towns and till very recently in most big cities, government offices of various kinds ranging from the post office to the police barracks provided the landmarks around which people laid out a map of their everyday lives and experiences. Often directions would be given with some government office in mind.

But in WORLP, only the office of the project director is a semi-permanent office, since it has been rented out from another governmental body. The offices of the block-level PIAs are operated in rented houses, and they frequently shift offices. Although WORLP is a government project, and its project holder the OWDM is a permanent body (a registered society) because of projectisation of the watershed development work, there is a thorough casualisation of work practices. Low-level functionaries are on periodic contracts, although some of them have served in various watershed development projects for nearly ten years now. They do not experience themselves as straightforward agents of the state. Due to these and other reasons, we argue that provisionalisation is one of the modes of fabricating the quotidian state, and the way in which 'the state' is seen and experienced comes to resemble 'transient' social actors such as NGOs and CBOs.

### Pluralisation of the State

Apart from the growing similarities in organisational culture and practices between GOs and NGOs, the state now seems to (a) lend itself to many appropriations on the ground and, therefore, to a certain kind of creative usage by population groups and (b) increasingly use multiple modalities and logics to justify and make sense of its actions. We identify a few of these logics and the modes of their imbrication.

**Participation** Participation provides one kind of logic that is increasingly being deployed to both justify and make sense of governmental action. The discourse over participation originated through the work of the social movements that sought, amongst other things, to expand the scope of citizenship rights (Cornwall and Brock 2005). But increasingly, multilateral agencies and governments are using this as an instrument of governance.

The postcolonial nation-state purportedly drew its legitimacy from two separate yet related modes of operation. The first mode was through the practice of electoral democracy in which the state claimed to represent the nation through the logic of representation. At the same time, it used the language of development to both create and operate on the domain of scientific planning to act upon society at a distance in its symbolic mode of fabrication. Social scientific work on India in particular and the global South in general has focused on the apparent contradictions between democracy and development.

With the increasing importance of the quotidian mode

of state fabrication, there seems to be an attempt to conflate these two logics through governmental technologies associated with participation. For example, in the village-level watershed committees of WORLP, tools for enabling participation are created with the logic of representation. Adequate representation of various population groups such as women, Scheduled Castes and Scheduled Tribes is aimed at.

**Targeting and Bhāg** With 'elite capture' increasingly framing narratives surrounding such morphing of the state, targeting is another logic that seems to be associated with modes of operation of state power. This is especially so in the field site of WORLP where the population in the project villages has been divided into four discrete groups with households as units—well-off, manageable, poor and very poor. Specific programmatic interventions are then targeted at each of these groups. The logic of targeting is premised upon a specific mode of governmentality that partitions people into distinct groups and then makes certain interventions contingent upon the membership of these groups. Participation then makes it possible for such targeting to happen by opening the project to the kind of scrutiny that it would not be subjected to otherwise. But targeting does not translate on the ground unmediated. The morphing of the state on the ground also makes for the infiltration of vernacular notions of politics into the domain of state action. The vernacular notion of bhg or reasonable share can be seen as one such logic.

### The Experience of Convergence

How the villagers saw the watershed staff did not vary much across the governmental and the NGO PIAs. Although the villagers saw 'watershed' as a government project, the way they related to and interacted with the watershed staff was different from their interactions with officials from other government departments. For example, almost all the members of the various watershed committees had the mobile number of the project director. They were often seen calling up the director even slightly late in the evening and discussing minute details of the work of the micro-watershed. This kind of access to a higher official would not be possible in most line departments and even villagers remark on this. On asking which department's staff visits their village the most, most villagers invariably reply that it is the 'watershed' staff that visits the most.

This familiarity seems to have resulted in contempt for the officials. For example, one often saw functionaries of the micro-watersheds complain about the PIA in a roundabout fashion to the project director when the same PIA has been around. Villagers do see 'watershed' as a government project, and they also act in a familiar fashion with the staff of the watershed mission. Thus, although the staff of the watershed mission were perceived and responded to differently from the response meted out to other line departments, there were significant similarities between the ways in which the staff of the GO and NGO PIA were dealt with by villagers and village-level functionaries of the project. This experience was characterised by an increasing familiarity between PIA-level and senior-level staff of the district watershed development mission.

In the preceding sections of this essay, we discussed the mission mode of 'doing government' and the attendant growth of the quotidian mode of state fabrication by looking at just one trope, that of growing *convergence* between the workings of governmental and non-governmental organisations. We teased out just a few of the aspects of such a process.

We posit this against the narratives surrounding political society that are increasingly becoming influential for understanding social change in the global South. Political society as a concept is of deeper theoretical provenance and can be seen as a mediating category that allows conversations between the rival schools of political economy and liberalism. The way Chatterjee uses political society is an intervention in the neo-Foucauldian literature on governmentality. But what is elided here is the fact that in the Foucauldian schema, although population seems like only an empirical category, it is in some sense a 'residue' of the theoretical enterprise of trying to understand the operations of disciplinary power. But Chatterjee takes population to be a more or less empirical category, and then makes an attempt at explaining how the politics of population groups congeal into the domain of political society.

Based on the discussions in the preceding sections, we argue that the understanding of the politics of population groups and the way they make claims and act upon the state can be better understood by trying to unpack the morphing within the body of the state. In our case, as already mentioned, this seems to be happening through the convergence of various types of organisations. To understand such a process, a state-in-society approach seems to be better suited as it is theoretically less overdetermined and allows us to make legible the messiness of everyday practice.

## NOTES

1. All the names used in this essay, apart from the name of the district and the project, are pseudonyms.

## REFERENCES

Baviskar, Amita and Nandini Sundar. 2008. 'Democracy versus Economic Transformation?', *Economic and Political Weekly*, 43(46): 87–89.

Chatterjee, Partha. 2008. 'Democracy and Economic Transformation in India', *Economic and Political Weekly*, 43(16): 53–62.

——. 2006 [2004]. *Politics of the Governed: Reflections on Popular Politics in Most of the World*: Delhi and Ranikhet: Permanent Black.

Cornwall, Andrea and Karen Brock. 2005. 'What Do Buzzwords Do for Development Policy? A Critical Look at "Participation", "Empowerment" and "Poverty Reduction"', *Third World Quarterly*, 26(7): 1043–1060.

Fuller, C. J. and John Harriss. 2000. 'For an Anthropology of the Modern Indian State', in C.J. Fuller and Véronique Bénéï (eds), *The Everyday State and Society in Modern India*. New Delhi: Social Science Press.

John, Mary E. and Satish Deshpande. 2008. 'Theorising the Present: Problems and Possibilities', *Economic and Political Weekly*, 43(46): 83–86.

Kamat, Sangeeta. 2002. *Development Hegemony: NGOs and the State in India*. New Delhi: Oxford University Press.

Migdal, Joel S. 2001. *State in Society: Studying How States and Societies Transform and Constitute One Another*. Cambridge: Cambridge University Press.

Shah, Mihir. 2008. 'Structures of Power in Indian Society: A Response', *Economic and Political Weekly*, 43(46): 78–83.

# 6
## INTERSTATE TRANSBOUNDARY WATER SHARING IN INDIA
### Conflict and Cooperation

*N. Shantha Mohan and Sailen Routray*

Water is no respecter of boundaries. Most of the larger rivers in India meander through the administrative boundaries of the Indian federal system. Sometimes, the river itself is the boundary, such as the Indravati which delineates the boundary between Maharashtra and Chhattisgarh for a part of its flow. Some rivers mark metaphorical boundaries as well—River Ganga serves as the vehicle to heaven, whereas the mythical River Vaitarani marks the crossing from this world of mortals to the infernal one. Therefore, in a fundamental sense, all rivers are transboundary in nature.

But for our somewhat mundane discussion, it is the wayward rivers that do not obey the diktats of human cartographic exercises that end up being marked and categorised as transboundary. For this discussion, the rivers that arise in one province in India but end up in another are termed as such. All the longer and major rivers in India are transboundary rivers: the Mahanadi originates in Amarkantak in Chhattisgarh and crosses over into Odisha before finding its way to the Bay of Bengal; the Chambal rises near Mhow in Madhya Pradesh before meandering for more than 900 kms to the Yamuna in Uttar Pradesh after having acquired a formidable reputation as the river of the badlands.

The Chambal is an example of a long river (with a length of around 960 kms) that complicates the ways in which rivers in India are clubbed together and categorised. It arises in the central highlands and drains into the River Yamuna which, in turn, joins the Ganges. Thus it forms part of the larger Gangetic river system. But it is difficult to locate it within the four-fold categorisation of rivers into Himalayan, peninsular, inland and small coastal ones flowing into the Arabian Sea.

The major Himalayan rivers are - Ganga, Yamuna, Son, Gandak, Brahmaputra, Lohit and Teesta. Large parts of the water that these Himalayan rivers receive is from the snowmelt during summer, and therefore, these are perennial in nature. Most of the larger rivers in peninsular India are east flowing, apart from a few exceptions such as the Narmada and Tapti that drain into the Arabian Sea. The important east-flowing rivers of peninsular India are - Subarnarekha, Mahanadi, Brahmani, Godavari, Krishna, Cauvery and Pennar. The Western Ghats form an important watershed for the southern part of the country. Apart from the several east-flowing rivers that originate here, many small and fast-flowing rivers such as Zuari, Mandovi, Netravati and Periyar originate here and, after flowing rapidly for a short distance, drain into the Arabian Sea. Several other rivers in India are transboundary. This is true both for larger rivers such as the Ganga and smaller rivers like Penner. Rivers such as Ghaggar and Luni do not find an outlet into the sea and lose their way in the desert wastes of Rajasthan and Gujarat.

Many transboundary rivers have significant implications for water usage and policymaking. In gross national terms, the availability of water can be termed comfortable. But this situation can change with increased demands due to the changing patterns of economic growth and urbanisation. Availability of water can greatly vary in terms of both spatial and temporal aspects. Spatially speaking, the northern and eastern parts of the country are better endowed as compared to the western and southern parts. The less endowed regions are the arid areas in the states of Rajasthan, Gujarat, Maharashtra, Karnataka, Andhra Pradesh and Tamil Nadu. They lie in one rain-shadow region or the other (Iyer 2003).

India has a monsoonal climate and the average annual rainfall is 1,170 mm. The annual rate varies from less than 150 mm per year in the northwestern extremities of the country to more than 10,000 mm per year of rainfall in Meghalaya. A large part of the country receives rain for only 100 hours a year. More than half the precipitation is received in a rainfall of less than about 20 hours (Agarwal et al. 1999). Therefore, storing water for later use is of utmost importance. It is this imperative to store water that creates the potential for conflicts over transboundary rivers.

As noted, with only 4 per cent of water resources of the world, India supports 16 per cent of the human and 15 per cent of the livestock population of the world. India gets around 4,000 billion cubic metres (BCM) of precipitation in an average year. Out of this, 3,000 BCM is received as rainfall in the summer monsoons spread over around 14 weeks, and the average annual water potential is around 1,869 BCM, out of which only 690 BCM can be harnessed due to hydrological and geological limitations. Replenishable groundwater resources are estimated at about 433 BCM. Thus, the total utilisable water potential stands at around 1,123 BCM. The utilisation now stands at around 605 BCM, out of which irrigation accounts for more than 80 per cent. Domestic, industrial, energy and other sectors consume around 30 BCM, 20 BCM, 20 BCM and 34 BCM respectively. The assured utilisable quantum of water of the country is around 1,123 BCM, whereas estimations of water needs for the year 2050 put this quantum at 1,447 BCM. The total storage capacity is 213 BCM from projects already completed. Storage capacity of around 76 BCM is under construction. Many corrective measures need to be taken for appropriate regulation and improvements in efficiencies. Due to the spiralling water demand, there is an increasing pressure to create storage facilities on rivers, of which most of the larger ones are interstate transboundary rivers (Jeyaseelan 2010).

## CONFLICT AND COOPERATION OVER TRANSBOUNDARY RIVERS IN INDIA

Several rivers in India flow across international and interstate boundaries, and many of these are sources of potential conflicts. But the experience around sharing of both international and interstate transboundary river waters is not all grim. The Indus Water Treaty between India and Pakistan that came out of a process of mediation, facilitated by the World Bank, is an important example of a working and successful resolution of disputes over an international transboundary river to which India was a party. The treaty awarded nearly 80 per cent of the water of the river system to Pakistan and 20 per cent to India. The treaty has survived three wars between the two countries, showing that such a treaty can weather even the worst of situations in a politically volatile region. The dispute between India and Bangladesh over the Ganga, especially the one surrounding the Farakka barrage was addressed with the signing of a thirty-year water-sharing treaty in 1996. This was an important step towards figuring out mechanisms for sharing the waters of other transboundary rivers between the two countries on a mutually acceptable basis (Mohan 2010).

Examples of successful dispute resolution in the case of river water sharing are to be found with regard to interstate transboundary rivers as well, such as the Damodar, Gandak and Subarnarekha. A salient example is the understanding reached on complex issues pertaining to the multi-basin and multipurpose Parambikulam–Aliyar Project, where a Joint Water Regulation Board has been established by the riparian states. But it must be mentioned here that these examples aside, there are many instances of interstate disputes over water sharing that face serious situations of potential conflict (Mohan 2010).

As the preceding discussions indicate, though India has a long history of cooperation over interstate transboundary rivers, its recent history is fraught with conflicts. There has been bitter fighting over the waters of Yamuna, Krishna and Cauvery.

The Yamuna is the longest tributary of the Ganges and is a vital source of water for irrigation and urban use in northern India. It feeds the northern states of Uttar Pradesh, Himachal Pradesh, Haryana, Rajasthan and Delhi. The total present claims on the river are more than twice the total water available. Its waters were shared between Uttar Pradesh and Punjab till 1954, when the new state of Haryana was created by slicing off a part of Punjab. Now Uttar Pradesh controls the Eastern Yamuna Canal and Haryana the Western Yamuna Canal. Following the rising demand from an explosively growing and urbanising state of Delhi, this arrangement was increasingly brought into question, leading to conflicts between Delhi, Haryana and Uttar Pradesh over the sharing of the Yamuna water, especially during the lean summer months. Matters have landed in the courts including the Supreme Court of India through the public interest litigation route. With water demand continuing to grow in the basin states, especially in Delhi, there is minimal chance of the dispute coming to a closure soon (Swain 2010).

In peninsular India, the Krishna waters have long been the cause of disputes. It is the second-longest river in the south and feeds the states of Maharashtra, Karnataka and Andhra Pradesh. The reorganisation of these states on a linguistic basis in the 1950s questioned the validity of the twenty-five-year agreement on Krishna (1951), which divided the river between the then Bombay, Hyderabad, Mysore and Madras states. The Krishna Dispute Tribunal headed by Justice Bachawat gave its award in 1976, asking the states to use their allocations by the year 2000. This led to a race for utilisation of the river`s water. One of the repercussions of such a process has been the growing demands and attendant conflicts, exemplified in the conflicts between Andhra Pradesh and Karnataka over the Almatti Dam in the latter state. The cause of the dispute was Karnataka`s decision to raise the height of the dam from its original 519 m to 524.25 m, a step that would have reduced the capacity of the Nagarjunasagar and Srisailam projects in Andhra Pradesh. But the two states were quick to join hands to oppose Maharashtra, the upper riparian state, when it tried to increase its storage capacity for the waters allocated to it. The states concerned have been complaining about each other to the central government over the issues. With increasing intensity of resource utilisation, such conflicts can only increase, since the overutilisation of waters of the Krishna river basin is about the highest in peninsular India (Swain 2010).

The Cauvery is another southern river whose waters have been the cause both of cooperation and conflict over a period of time. The regions of the present-day Tamil Nadu were the first movers in using the water of the river. Before the growth of modern dam-building technologies, the upland areas, which today is the state of Karnataka, used very little of its waters. In the latter half of the nineteenth century, attempts by the then Mysore princely state to dam and use the waters of the Cauvery River led to protests from the Madras Presidency of the British Raj. Negotiations between the two followed, and a treaty was signed in 1892. This agreement put on record the projects already taken up and laid down that the Government of Mysore will undertake no new projects. When Mysore proposed the construction of the Krishnaraja Sagar Dam on the Cauvery, the Madras Government challenged the decision and sent a complaint to the arbitration committee set up under the agreement of 1892. On receiving an unfavourable judgment from the committee, the Government of Madras took the matter to the secretary of state in 1919 and got a favourable response. Soon after this, matters were again taken up for negotiation between the two governments and a fifty-year agreement was reached in 1924. This agreement allowed the construction of the Krishnaraja Sagar Dam in the then Mysore state and the Mettur Dam in Madras Presidency. It also provided a framework for the development of irrigation in the Cauvery Basin. This agreement was supposed to be renewed after fifty years, that is, in 1974, but this was not done. This fifty-year period saw the intensification of irrigation development in Karnataka and Tamil Nadu, the successors of the princely state of Mysore and the British Indian province of Madras respectively. The increase in the intensive use of water, especially for irrigation, led to conflicts. Tamil Nadu, which had enjoyed the advantage of being the first mover in irrigation development, now started complaining about the overuse of the waters of the Cauvery by Karnataka, the upper riparian state. It started demanding the creation of a tribunal for the resolution of these disputes and sharing of the waters of Cauvery. In 1990, the Cauvery Water Disputes Tribunal was set up, which came out with its award in 2007. The Government of Karnataka was dissatisfied with the award (Settar 2010).

## RULES AND MECHANISMS TO ADDRESS TRANSBOUNDARY WATER SHARING IN INDIA

The foregoing section shows that the history of interstate river water sharing has been characterised by both cooperation and conflict. Water conflicts are of many types, depending on the perspectives of the contesting parties and the nature of the contest. The complexity of the issues is exacerbated by the deficiencies in the legal and institutional mechanisms. Irrigation as a sector consumes more than 80 per cent of all available water in the country. Listed as Enry 17 under the State List in the Constitution, it is subject to the provisions of Entry 56 of the Union List. The latter empowers the central government to legislate on interstate river issues. But this entry has been underused. Article 262 of the Constitution provides for an adjudication role by the centre in these conflicts. The Inter-State Water Disputes Act (ISWD), 1956 was promulgated under Article 262. This Act provides for the formation of tribunals for settling transboundary river disputes (Mohan 2010).

According to the provisions of the ISWD Act, a state government having a dispute with another over interstate river waters can ask the centre to set up a tribunal for adjudication. But the efficacy of tribunals to settle such disputed rivers is coming increasingly under question. There have been substantial problems surrounding the tribunals set up to settle the disputes over the waters of Ravi–Beas and Cauvery. The awards in both the cases have failed to resolve the disputes and have led to further bouts of intense politicking. The tribunal's award now has the status of the decree of the Supreme Court, by virtue of the recent amendments to the ISWD Act. The tribunals take a lot of time to reach a final settlement. Even the amended Act of 2002 mandates a time limit of six years. But even six years is, relatively speaking, a long period of time to resolve such issues. In this context, a mention must be made of several non-official civil society efforts that have been working assiduously to address the issues concerning river water sharing. The Madras Institute of Development Studies (MIDS), Chennai, initiated the setting up of a platform to facilitate dialoguing between the farmers of Karnataka and Tamil Nadu in the Cauvery Basin. Thus, by talking to each other, the farmers have begun to understand each other's problems and needs (Mohan 2010).

## ADDRESSING TRANSBOUNDARY WATER CONFLICTS

In this context, we list some ways that can be of help in addressing issues of transboundary water conflicts. The first path is of an institutional nature. We suggest that the already existing institutions, as also the formation of new institutions, such as river basin organisations (RBOs) can go some distance in resolving water conflicts. We also need to use some new tools or use old ones differently to be able to deal with water conflicts creatively. In this regard, we list mediation and an alternative approach to scenario building as two possible ways.

### The Inter-State Council

Article 263 of the Constitution envisages the establishment of an Inter-State Council (ISC) with the mandate to enquire into and give advice on disputes arising between states, to investigate subjects of common interest to them and to offer recommendations for better coordination of policy and action. The Administrative Reforms Commission (1969), the Rajamannar Committee (1971) and the Sarkaria Commission (1983) in their reports recommended the setting up of the ISC. The ISC was finally established by a Presidential Order on the 28th of May, 1990, as a recommendatory body to fulfil its constitutional mandate. The council comprises the prime minister, all chief ministers, administrators of union territories, six ministers of the central cabinet as also permanent invitees. The ISC secretariat, which provides organisational support to the council, is headed by a secretary who is also the secretary of the Commission on Centre–State Relations. He is assisted by two advisers and additional secretaries.

Conducting relevant studies is also a mandatory task of the ISC. Studies have already been commissioned on providing compensation to resource-bearing states; sub-national governance; and an appraisal of measures taken to implement the Directive Principles of State Policy. The council provides a forum for discussions on complex public policy and governance issues having a bearing on centre–state relations or having interstate dimensions. Since the council is a statutory body and has now built a body of experience in dealing with matters that are of common interest to states, it can play a useful role in facilitating dialogues and discussions towards resolving conflicts surrounding transboundary water sharing in the country (Iyer 2002, Mohan 2010, ISC 2010).

### River Basin Organisations

There is a need to look at arbitration and negotiations as methods of conflict resolution. One institutional arrangement that can be used to facilitate negotiation surrounding interstate rivers is the RBO. RBOs can be set up under the River Boards Act of 1956 (RBA), which was legislated under Article 56 of the Union List. These are empowered to regulate and develop interstate rivers and their basins. The board is required to have members with expertise in irrigation, water and soil conservation, and finance. But river boards have not been established because state governments apprehend that the boards would impinge upon their authority and power (Iyer 2007). However, in this era of coalition politics, states have started seeing the advantage as also the need to set up RBOs.

### Mediation as a Method for Dealing with Transboundary Water Conflicts

To date, seven tribunals have been established to deal with disputes over the waters of transboundary rivers. But these have not always helped to resolve the disputes in a satisfactory manner. These tribunals depend on legal principles of arbitration. Their awards, although supposedly final and binding, have been challenged in courts, and the courts have entertained these challenges. The judicial process is essentially an adversarial process and damages the relationship between the disputants. In contrast, mediation is a process that employs a neutral person or persons to facilitate a process of negotiations between the disputing parties so as to arrive at a mutually acceptable solution. Mediators should not have any direct interest in the conflict or have control over the process of mediation and its outcomes. The power is vested with the disputants, but the mediation process is flexible and informal and can draw upon the multidisciplinary perspectives of the mediators. On the subcontinental level, the World Bank played the role of mediator between India and Pakistan and succeeded in resolving the conflicts surrounding the rivers of the Indus Basin. In the Zambezi River dispute, the Vatican negotiated to fruition an eleven-nation agreement for the joint use and management of the river`s waters (Devi 2010).

Given these examples, there is an urgent need in India to deploy mediation as a tool for conflict resolution and participatory management.

### Alternative Approaches to Scenario Building for Water

The manner in which scenario building in the water sector takes place reduced it to a mere 'technical` tool for prediction. Scenario building is not a tool for projection and need not be used as one. A scenario is essentially an imaginative exercise involving political and social choices. It is as much a tool for action as it is for thought.

While undertaking exercises of scenario building, one needs to take into account the physical qualities of water as a resource. Generally, in such exercises, the current patterns of consumption are taken for granted to arrive at projections of various likely demands in the future. Thus, these attempts are just tunnel vision exercises based on the current patterns to project possible future demands. We argue that there is a need for a completely different way of building scenarios. We need to hypothetically freeze the total available water or freeze the quantum at current levels of total consumption in a given region–the unit for analysis–and build scenarios of alternative usage patterns. Thus, building a scenario should not be taken as merely predicting the total quantum of water that would be in demand at a future date. What one can alternatively do is plan as if water, and its characteristics as a life-giving resource, mattered. This will necessarily be a non-technocratic and democratic exercise, since what one is trying to simulate in this proposed alternative method is the social choices that we might want to make if water availability and/or consumption were to be frozen at some arbitrary point in the present. Such an exercise will help us unravel the assumptions that we make while making projections. Such an approach will also help us radically interrogate theories of risk society by positing scenarios as 'designs` (Routray 2010).

Water is becoming an increasingly important site of contestation among the states in India because of the rapid rates of population and economic growth and because of increasing urbanisation. The growing importance of coalitions at the national level and the related assertion of regional identities add to the intractability of the problems surrounding transboundary water sharing in India. More often than not, such issues are a result of the focus on demand-side management. Many scholars have argued that emphasising supply-side management might be one way of dealing with such issues. There is a lot of merit in this argument. But we need to undertake institutional innovations as well. The suggestions for setting up RBOs and giving a greater role to the ISC in dealing with interstate river issues should be given due consideration. With the changing political dynamics in the country, it should not be difficult to convince the states that the relationship between governments at the level of the states and at the centre is not a zero-sum game. Increasing roles for central institutions in dealing with issues emerging out of sharing the waters of the transboundary rivers does not necessarily mean a whittling down of the powers of the states. Second, as this essay has argued, one needs to creatively use the already existing tools (such as mediation and scenario-building exercises) for managing water resources of interstate rivers more effectively and democratically. The emergent solutions have to be context specific and have to borrow creatively from a bouquet of solutions.

## REFERENCES

Agarwal, Anil, Sunita Narain and Srabani Sen (eds). 1999. *The State of India's Environment: The Citizen's Fifth Report*. New Delhi: Centre for Science and Environment.

Devi, Geetha M. 2010. 'Legal Framework for Resolution of Water Disputes`, paper presented at the National Consultation on Water Conflicts in India: The State, the People and the Future, 15–16

March, National Institute of Advanced Studies, Bangalore.

Inter-State Council (ISC). 2010. http://interstatecouncil.nic.in/, accessed on 1st of September, 2011.

Iyer, Ramaswamy. 2007. *Towards Water Wisdom: Limits, Justice, Harmony*. New Delhi: Sage Publications.

——. 2003. *Water: Perspectives, Issues, Concerns*. New Delhi, Thousand Oaks and London: Sage Publications.

——. 2002. 'Inter-State Water Disputes Act 1956: Difficulties and Solutions', *Economic and Political Weekly*, 37(28): 2907–2910.

Jeyaseelan, R. 2010. 'Regulatory Aspects in Water Resources Development and Management', in Shantha Mohan, Sailen Routray and N. Shashikumar (eds), *River Water Sharing: Transboundary Conflict and Cooperation in India,* pp. 81–95. New Delhi: Routledge.

Mohan, Shantha N. 2010. 'Locating Transboundary Water Sharing in India', in N. Shantha Mohan, Sailen Routray and N. Shashikumar (eds), *River Water Sharing: Transboundary Conflict and Cooperation in India,* pp. 3–22. New Delhi: Routledge.

Routray, Sailen. 2010. 'Water Conflicts and Scenario Building in Orissa: An Alternative Approach', paper presented at Orissa Environmental Congress, 22–24 December, Regional Museum of Natural History, Bhubaneswar.

Settar, S. 2010. 'Kaveri in Its Historical Setting', in N. Shantha Mohan, Sailen Routray and N. Shashikumar (eds), *River Water Sharing: Transboundary Conflict and Cooperation in India,* pp. 99–107. New Delhi: Routledge.

Swain, A. 2010. *Struggle against the State: Social Network and Protest Mobilization in India*. Farnham and Burlington: Ashgate.

# INDEX